First World War
and Army of Occupation
War Diary
France, Belgium and Germany

21 DIVISION
Divisional Troops
97 Field Company Royal Engineers
11 September 1915 - 29 April 1919

WO95/2144/1

The Naval & Military Press Ltd
www.nmarchive.com
Published in association with The National Archives

Published by

The Naval & Military Press Ltd

Unit 10 Ridgewood Industrial Park,

Uckfield, East Sussex,

TN22 5QE England

Tel: +44 (0) 1825 749494

www.naval-military-press.com

www.nmarchive.com

This diary has been reprinted in facsimile from the original. Any imperfections are inevitably reproduced and the quality may fall short of modern type and cartographic standards.

© Crown Copyright
Images reproduced by permission of The National Archives, London, England, 2015.

Contents

Document type	Place/Title	Date From	Date To
Heading	WO95/2144/1 97 Field Company Royal Engineers		
Heading	21st Division 97th Field Coy R.E. Sep 1915-Apr 1919		
Heading	21st Division 97th F.C.R.E. Vol I Sept 15		
Heading	War Diary Of 97th Field Company 21st Div. From 11.9.15 to 30.9.15 Vol. 1		
War Diary	Havre	11/09/1915	11/09/1915
War Diary	St. Omer	12/09/1915	12/09/1915
War Diary	Ganspette	13/09/1915	20/09/1915
War Diary	Wittes	21/09/1915	21/09/1915
War Diary	Lespresses	21/09/1915	22/09/1915
War Diary	Rambert	22/09/1915	24/09/1915
War Diary	Noeux Les Mines	24/09/1915	25/09/1915
War Diary	Noyelles les Vermelles	25/09/1915	25/09/1915
War Diary	2000 S.E. of above.	26/09/1915	28/09/1915
War Diary	Bethune	29/09/1915	29/09/1915
War Diary	Estree Blanche	30/09/1915	30/09/1915
Heading	21st Division 97th F.C.R.E. Vol 2 Oct 15		
Heading	War Diary Of 97th Field Company R.E. From 1.10.15 To 31-10-15 Vol. I.		
War Diary	Estree Blanche	01/10/1915	01/10/1915
War Diary	Steenbecque	01/10/1915	02/10/1915
War Diary	Strazeele	02/10/1915	10/10/1915
War Diary	Armentieres	10/10/1915	31/10/1915
Heading	21st Division 97th F.C.R.E. Vol 3 Nov 15		
Heading	War Diary of 97th Field Coy R.E. from 1.11.15 to 30.11.15 (Volume 3)		
War Diary	Armentieres	01/11/1915	30/11/1915
Heading	21st 97th F.C.R.E. Vol. 4		
Heading	War Diary Of 97th Field Coy. Royal Engineers From 1st December 1915 To 31st December 1915 (Volume 4).		
Heading	War Diary Of 97th Field Coy R.E. From December 1st 1915 to December 31st 1915 (Volume 4).		
War Diary	Armentiers	01/12/1915	30/12/1915
Heading	21st Divisional Engineers 97th Field Company R.E. January 1916		
Heading	War Diary Of 97th Field Coy R.E. From January 1st 1916 to January 31st 1916 (Volume 5)		
War Diary	Armentiers	01/01/1916	31/01/1916
Heading	21st Divisional Engineers 97th Field Company R.E. February 1916		
War Diary	War Diary Of 97th Field Coy R.E. From 1st February To 29th February 1916 (Volume 6)		
War Diary	Armentiers	01/02/1916	29/02/1916
Heading	21st Divisional Engineers 97th Field Company R.E. March 1916		
War Diary	Armentieres	01/03/1916	30/03/1916
War Diary	Bailleul	31/03/1916	31/03/1916
Heading	21st Divisional Engineers 97th Field Company R.E. April 1916		

Heading	War Diary Of 97th Field Coy R.E. from April 1st 1916 to April 30th. 1916 (Volume 8).		
War Diary	Longueau	01/04/1916	01/04/1916
War Diary	Cardonnette	02/04/1916	08/04/1916
War Diary	Bonnay	09/04/1916	18/04/1916
War Diary	Ville	19/04/1916	30/04/1916
Heading	21st Divisional Engineers 97th Field Company R.E. May 1916		
Heading	War Diary Of 97th Field Coy R.E. from May 1st 1916 to May 31st 1916		
War Diary	Ville	01/05/1916	31/05/1916
Heading	21st Divisional Engineers 97th Field Company R.E. June 1916		
Heading	War Diary Of 97th Field Coy R.E. From June 1st 1916 To June 30th 1916 (Volume. 10).		
War Diary	Ville	01/06/1916	30/06/1916
Heading	21st Divisional Engineers 97th Field Company R.E. July 1916		
Heading	War Diary Of 97th Field Co. R.E. July 1916		
War Diary	Becourtvalley	01/07/1916	04/07/1916
War Diary	Becourt	04/07/1916	05/07/1916
War Diary	Argoeuvres	06/07/1916	07/07/1916
War Diary	Saisseval	08/07/1916	10/07/1916
War Diary	Ville	11/07/1916	11/07/1916
War Diary	Becourtvalley	12/07/1916	14/07/1916
War Diary	South of Fricourt wood	15/07/1916	18/07/1916
War Diary	Buire	19/07/1916	19/07/1916
War Diary	Allonville	20/07/1916	22/07/1916
War Diary	Longueau St Pol	23/07/1916	23/07/1916
War Diary	Ternas	24/07/1916	28/07/1916
War Diary	Givenchy	25/07/1916	25/07/1916
War Diary	Le-Noble	25/07/1916	28/07/1916
War Diary	Arras	29/07/1916	31/07/1916
Heading	21st Divisional Engineers 97th Field Company R.E. August 1916		
War Diary	Arras	01/08/1916	31/08/1916
Heading	21st Divisional Engineers 97th Field Company R.E. September 1916		
Heading	War Diary Of 97th Field Coy. R.E. from September 1st 1916 to September 30th 1916 (Volume 13).		
War Diary	Arras	01/09/1916	04/09/1916
War Diary	Noyellette	05/09/1916	05/09/1916
War Diary	Sombrin	06/09/1916	12/09/1916
War Diary	Authie	13/09/1916	13/09/1916
War Diary	Dernancourt	14/09/1916	15/09/1916
War Diary	Becordel Camp	16/09/1916	16/09/1916
War Diary	North of Bernafay Wood	17/09/1916	30/09/1916
Heading	21st Divisional Engineers 97th Field Company R.E. October 1916		
War Diary	N of bernafay Wood	02/10/1916	11/10/1916
War Diary	Noyelles Les Vermelles	12/10/1916	31/10/1916
Miscellaneous	62nd Infantry Brigade Approximate Programme of Work for 97th Field Coy. R.E.	22/10/1916	22/10/1916
Heading	21st Divisional Engineers 97th Field Company R.E. November 1916		

Heading	War Diary Of 97th Field Co R.E. From 1st Nov 1916 To 30th Nov 1916		
War Diary	Noyelles Les Vermelles	01/11/1916	30/11/1916
Miscellaneous	Additional Work Programme.	10/11/1916	10/11/1916
Heading	21st Divisional Engineers 97th Field Company R.E. December 1916		
Heading	War Diary Of 97th Field Coy R.E. for December 1st 1916 to December 31st 1916 (Volume 16)		
War Diary	Noyelles Les Vermelles	01/12/1916	26/12/1916
War Diary	Marles Les Mines	27/12/1916	31/12/1916
Heading	War Diary Of 97th (Field) Co R.E. From Jan 1 1917 To Jan 31 1917		
War Diary	Marles Les Mines	01/01/1917	31/01/1917
Heading	War Diary Of 97th Field Co. R.E. 21st Division 1st 28th Feb 1917		
War Diary	G Camp Poperinghe	01/02/1917	15/02/1917
War Diary	Bethune	16/02/1917	17/02/1917
War Diary	Noyellrs	18/02/1917	28/02/1917
Heading	War Diary Of 97th Field Co. R.E. 21st Div. March 1st to 31st. 1917 Vol. XIX		
War Diary	Rubecq	28/02/1917	02/03/1917
War Diary	Gonnehem	03/03/1917	09/03/1917
War Diary	Fontaine	10/03/1917	10/03/1917
War Diary	Monneville	11/03/1917	11/03/1917
War Diary	Hautecut	12/03/1917	12/03/1917
War Diary	Halloy	14/03/1917	31/03/1917
Heading	War Diary Of 97th Field Co R.E. Vol XX. 1-30 April 1917		
War Diary	Boiry St Martin	01/04/1917	26/04/1917
War Diary	Boiry Becquerelle	27/04/1917	30/04/1917
Map	Survey of Strong Points. No. 6 to 15		
Miscellaneous	Work to be done by 97th Co. R.E. D. Coy. Pioneers.		
Heading	War Diary Of 97th Field Co. R.E. May 1917 Vol 21		
War Diary	Boiry Becquerelle	01/05/1917	12/05/1917
War Diary	Ransart	13/05/1917	31/05/1917
Map	Sheet-516 S.W. Scale 1:20,000		
Heading	War Diary Of 97 Field Co. R.E. June 1-30 1917		
War Diary	Judas Farm	01/06/1917	17/06/1917
War Diary	Nr St Leger	18/06/1917	26/06/1917
War Diary	Bellacourt	27/06/1917	30/06/1917
War Diary	Boiry Becquerelle	01/07/1917	01/07/1917
Diagram etc	Base Line 313 M		
Diagram etc	Plan Of Dugout Constructed By The 97th F. Coy. R.E. June 1917		
Heading	War Diary Of 97th Field Co R.E. 1st-31st July 1917		
War Diary	Boiry-Becquerelle	01/07/1917	31/07/1917
Miscellaneous	Programme Of Work	07/07/1917	07/07/1917
Miscellaneous	Programme Of Work	16/07/1917	16/07/1917
Heading	War Diary of 97th Field Co. R E. August-1st-31st 1917		
War Diary	Hamelincourt	01/08/1917	27/08/1917
War Diary	Dainville	28/08/1917	31/08/1917
Heading	War Diary of 97th Field Co RE Septr. 1917		
War Diary	Dainville	01/09/1917	07/09/1917
War Diary	Ridge Wood	08/09/1917	30/09/1917
War Diary	Ridge Wood	19/09/1917	22/09/1917
Heading	War Diary Of 97th Field Co RE 1st-31st Oct. 1917		

War Diary	Ridge Wood	01/10/1917	16/10/1917
War Diary	Mille Kruis	17/10/1917	25/10/1917
War Diary	Elzenwalle Chateau	26/10/1917	31/10/1917
Miscellaneous	C.R.E. 31st Div.	03/10/1917	03/10/1917
War Diary	Elzenwalle Chateau	01/11/1917	14/11/1917
War Diary	West Outre	15/11/1917	16/11/1917
War Diary	Doulieu	17/11/1917	17/11/1917
War Diary	Gonneheim	18/11/1917	18/11/1917
War Diary	Coupigny	19/11/1917	19/11/1917
War Diary	Mt. St. Eloy	20/11/1917	20/11/1917
War Diary	Ecurie Area	21/11/1917	22/11/1917
War Diary	G. 3d. 2.2 Sheet 57B.	23/11/1917	30/11/1917
War Diary	Marueuil Station	01/12/1917	01/12/1917
War Diary	Brusle	02/12/1917	16/12/1917
War Diary	Epehy	17/12/1917	21/12/1917
War Diary	Liekamont	22/12/1917	31/12/1917
Heading	21st Div. War Diary 97th Field Company, R.E. March (1/23.3.18) 1918		
War Diary	Lieramont	01/03/1918	23/03/1918
Heading	21st Divisional Engineers 97th Field Company R.E. April 1918		
War Diary	Hangest-Sur Somme	01/04/1918	02/04/1918
War Diary	Locre	03/04/1918	04/04/1918
War Diary	R.E. Farm	05/04/1918	10/04/1918
War Diary	Chateau Segard	11/04/1918	16/04/1918
War Diary	Ouderdom	17/04/1918	25/04/1918
War Diary	Ouderdom (G 24 b 33)	26/04/1918	30/04/1918
War Diary	Ouderdom	01/05/1918	01/05/1918
War Diary	Poperinghe	02/05/1918	02/05/1918
War Diary	Steenvoorde	03/05/1918	03/05/1918
War Diary	Lederzeele	04/05/1918	04/05/1918
War Diary	On Rail	05/05/1918	05/05/1918
War Diary	Serzy Savigny	06/05/1918	06/05/1918
War Diary	Anthenay	07/05/1918	12/05/1918
War Diary	Lhery	13/05/1918	13/05/1918
War Diary	Prouilly	14/05/1918	14/05/1918
War Diary	Chalons Le Verguer	15/05/1918	27/05/1918
War Diary	Branscourt	28/05/1918	28/05/1918
War Diary	Ville En Tardenois	29/05/1918	29/05/1918
War Diary	Marfaux	30/05/1918	30/05/1918
War Diary	Forest D'Epernay	31/05/1918	31/05/1918
War Diary	Soulieres	01/06/1918	03/06/1918
War Diary	Villevenard	04/06/1918	09/06/1918
War Diary	Beauvais La Noue	10/06/1918	14/06/1918
War Diary	Sezanne	15/06/1918	15/06/1918
War Diary	Hallencourt	16/06/1918	16/06/1918
War Diary	St Aubin Riviere	17/06/1918	21/06/1918
War Diary	Soreng	22/06/1918	22/06/1918
War Diary	Bethencourt	23/06/1918	01/07/1918
War Diary	Beauquesne	02/07/1918	19/07/1918
War Diary	Clairfaye Farm	20/07/1918	24/07/1918
War Diary	Forceville	24/07/1918	25/07/1918
War Diary	Beaussart	26/07/1918	24/08/1918
War Diary	Auchonvillers	25/08/1918	25/08/1918
War Diary	Battery Valley Near Grandcourt	26/08/1918	04/09/1918
War Diary	Le Sars	05/09/1918	05/09/1918

War Diary	Morval	06/09/1918	07/09/1918
War Diary	Manancourt	08/09/1918	24/09/1918
War Diary	Heudicourt	25/09/1918	30/09/1918
Heading	War Diary Of 97th (Field) Company., Royal Engineers. From Oct. 1st. To Oct. 31st. 1918		
War Diary	Heudecourt	01/10/1918	05/10/1918
War Diary	Gonnelieu	06/10/1918	10/10/1918
War Diary	Walincourt	11/10/1918	18/10/1918
War Diary	Audencourt	19/10/1918	22/10/1918
War Diary	Neuvilly	23/10/1918	29/10/1918
War Diary	Poix Du Nord	30/10/1918	31/10/1918
Heading	War Diary Of 97 (Field) Co RE Month-November 1918 Vol XXXIX		
War Diary	Poix Du Nord	01/11/1918	05/11/1918
War Diary	Locquignol	06/11/1918	07/11/1918
War Diary	Latete Noire	08/11/1918	08/11/1918
War Diary	Berlaimont	09/11/1918	30/11/1918
Heading	War Diary Of 97 (Field) Coy RE Month Of December 1918		
War Diary	Berlaimont	01/12/1918	01/12/1918
War Diary	Engelfontaine	02/12/1918	02/12/1918
War Diary	Amiens	03/12/1918	03/12/1918
War Diary	Cavillon	04/12/1918	31/12/1918
Heading	War Diary Of 97th (Field) Company R.E. From 1st January 1919 To 31st January 1919		
War Diary	Oissy	01/01/1919	31/01/1919
Heading	War Diary Of 97th (Field) Company., R.E. From 1st February 1919 To 28th February, 1919		
War Diary	In The Field	01/02/1919	14/02/1919
War Diary	Oissy	15/02/1919	04/04/1919
War Diary	Long Le Catelet	05/04/1919	25/04/1919
War Diary	Havre	26/04/1919	29/04/1919
Miscellaneous	97th (Field) Company R.E.		

WO95/2144/1

97 Field Company
Royal Engineers

21ST DIVISION

97TH FIELD COY R.E.
SEP 1915-APR 1919

21st Khwaim

97th 2.C.R.E.
Vol I
Sept. 15

12/7/21

Confidential

War Diary
of
97th Field Company 21st Div.

from 11.9.15   to 30-9-15.

Vol. 1.

H. Syme
Capt R.E.
O.C. 97 Coy R.E.

Army Form C. 2118

WAR DIARY
or
INTELLIGENCE SUMMARY.

(Erase heading not required.)

1915

Place	Date	Hour	Summary of Events and Information	Remarks and references to Appendices
HAVRE	11.9	9 a.m.	Disembarked from three ships and proceeded to No 5 Rest Camp.	W.S.
"		9 p.m.	Entrained at Gare des Marchandises	W.S.
CRONER	12.9	5.15 p.m.	Detrained and marched to bivouac at GANSPETTE	W.S.
GANSPETTE	13.9		Rest. Move into billets	W.S.
"	14.9		Continue Training	W.S.
"	15.9		"	
"	16.9		"	

W.S.S. Lt Captn R.E.
7° O.C. 97 M^7 Co R.E.

WAR DIARY
INTELLIGENCE SUMMARY.

Army Form C. 2118

1915

Place	Date	Hour	Summary of Events and Information	Remarks and references to Appendices
ANSPETTE	17.9.15		Continue Training	
"	18.9		"	H.S.
"	19.9	6 p.m.	"	H.S.
"	20.9	6 p.m.	Parade and move off in 62nd I.B. group	H.S.
NITTES	21.9	12.50 a.m.	Go into bivouac	
"	"	7.15 p.m.	Parade and move off in 62nd I.B. group	H.S.
SPRESSES	"	11.30 p.m.	Go into billet and bivouac	
"	22.9	7 p.m.	Parade and move off in 62nd I.B. group	H.S.
AMBERT	"	10.30 p.m.	Go into billet and bivouac	H.S.
"	23.9	—	Rest.	
"	24.9	6 p.m.	Parade and move off in 62nd I.B. group	

Army Form C. 2118

WAR DIARY
or
INTELLIGENCE SUMMARY.
(Erase heading not required).

Instructions regarding War Diaries and Intelligence Summaries are contained in F. S. Regs., Part II. and the Staff Manual respectively. Title pages will be prepared in manuscript.

Place	Date	Hour	Summary of Events and Information	Remarks and references to Appendices
NOEUX les MINES	24.9	11 p.m.	Go into bivouac	
"	25.9	10:30 a.m.	Parade and march to NOYELLES les VERMELLES	A.S.
NOYELLES les VERMELLES	25.9	5 p.m.	Parade & march 2000× S.E. on main road. Go into billet and bivouac. Receive orders that 21st Div. forms part of Gen. reserve for attack. Orders for 21st Div. leas 62nd I.B. to attack. 62nd I.B. but to 15th Div. Coy. in Div. reserve.	A.S.
		8 p.m.		
2000× S.E. of above	26.9.	by day	One section repairing roads and one improving communications in ground captured.	A.S.
		by night	Parade 5.45 p.m. and march to trenches with three bridging wagon loads of wire and sandbags, with orders to report to G.O.C. 64th I.B. Return at dawn not having found 64th I.B.	
"	27.9		rest	
"	28.9	8.55 a.m.	Parade and march to BETHUNE by devious route	A.S.
BETHUNE	29.9	4.30 p.m.	Go into billet and bivouac	

H.S. Ward Capt R.E.
for O.C. 97 Coy R.E.

1915.

Army Form C. 2118

WAR DIARY
or
INTELLIGENCE SUMMARY.

Place	Date	Hour	Summary of Events and Information	Remarks and references to Appendices
BETHUNE	29.9	4 p.m.	Parade and march to ESTREE BLANCHE	K.S.
ESTREE BLANCHE	30.9	2 a.m.	Go into billet and bivouac.	
"	1.10	6 a.m.	Parade and march to STEENBECQUE	
STEENBECQUE	"	11 a.m.	Go into billet and bivouac.	
"	2.10	7.15 a.m.	Parade and march to 62nd F.A. group to STRAZEELE	

H.S.V. Capt R.E.
for O.C. 97 F.Ry Co.

D/7595

21st Hussars

97th F.C. R.E.
Vol A
Oct 15

CONFIDENTIAL

War Diary
of
97th Field Company R.E.

from 1·10·15 to 31-10-15

Vol. I

Army Form C. 2118.

WAR DIARY
INTELLIGENCE SUMMARY.
(Erase heading not required.)

10/15

Instructions regarding War Diaries and Intelligence Summaries are contained in F. S. Regs., Part II. and the Staff Manual respectively. Title pages will be prepared in manuscript.

Place	Date	Hour	Summary of Events and Information	Remarks and references to Appendices
ESTREE BLANCHE	1.10	6 a.m.	Parade and march to STEENBECQUE	H.Q.
STEENBECQUE	"	11 a.m.	Go into billet and bivouac	H.Q.
"	2.10	7.45 a.m.	Parade and march in 62nd I.B. group to STRAZEELE	H.Q.
STRAZEELE	2.10	11 a.m.	Go into billet and bivouac	H.Q.
"	3.10	—	Refit.	H.Q.
"	4.10	—	Draw stores from R.E. Park and continue training, hand wagons & clean tools	
"	5.10	—	"	
"	6.10	—	Continue training, clean tools & repair wagons.	
"	7.10	—	"	
"	8.10	—	"	
"	9.10	8.30	Ordered to parade. Parade cancelled 8 a.m. Company ordered to be ready to move at 2 hours notice.	

Army Form C. 2118.

WAR DIARY
or
INTELLIGENCE SUMMARY.
(Erase heading not required.)

Place	Date	Hour	Summary of Events and Information	Remarks and references to Appendices
STRAZEELE	10.10	12.15 pm	Parade and march to ARMENTIERES	H.S.
ARMENTIE-RES	"	5.30 pm	Go into billets in Tram Power station in 50th Div. Area.	
"	11.10	—	Clean billets. Officers go round work to be done.	H.S.
"	12.10	—	Commence work on 2nd line just N. of River Lys. One company of Pioneers allotted to us for work. Extending farms, sinking but wire entanglements, and improving existing trenches.	H.S.
"	13.10	—	Continue work as above	
"	14.10	"	ditto	
"	15.10	"	ditto. No 1 Section proceeds to ~~Rennes~~ MERRIS for work under Div. H.Q.	
"	16.10	"	ditto	
"	17.10	"	ditto	

Army Form C. 2118.

WAR DIARY
or
INTELLIGENCE SUMMARY.
(Erase heading not required)

Instructions regarding War Diaries and Intelligence Summaries are contained in F. S. Regs., Part II. and the Staff Manual respectively. Title pages will be prepared in manuscript.

Place	Date	Hour	Summary of Events and Information	Remarks and references to Appendices
ARMENTIERES	18·10	—	Continue work on 2nd Line defences (see above) especially Farm buildings	HSC
"	19·10	—	ditto	HSC
"	20·10	—	ditto	HSC
"	21·10	—	"	HSC
"	22·10	—	"	HSC
"	23·10	—	"	HSC
"	24·10	—	"	
"	25·10	—	"	
"	26·10	—	"	
"	27·10	—	" Moved one section to an adjacent house for billeting, owing to water in Tramway basement	HSC
"	28·10	—	" Moved another section to different billet for same reason.	HSC
"	29·10	—	"	
"	30·10	—	"	
"	31·10	—	"	

HSyCampbell.
for OC 97 Field Co RE.

97th R.E.
Vol 3

21/7678

21st Kumaun

Nov 15

LN

Confidential

War Diary
of
97th Field Coy R.E.

from 1.11.15 to 30.11.15.

(Volume. 3.)

Army Form C. 2118.

WAR DIARY
or
INTELLIGENCE SUMMARY.
(Erase heading not required.)

of 97 Fd Co R E November 1915

Place	Date	Hour	Summary of Events and Information	Remarks and references to Appendices
Montiers	1.11.15	Nos 2, 3 & 4 Sections Continue work on Subsidiary line North of the LYS especially Farms LYS & La FLANGUE	
	2.11		ditto	
	3.11		ditto	
	4.11		ditto	
	5.11		ditto The Company to take over work on the front line trenches 79-80 as from 6. pm 5.11.15.	
	6.11		Commenced revetting trenches 74-80 No 2 Sect 74 75 76 / 3 " 77 78 / 4 " 79 80	
			Commenced making H revetting frames & dugouts in billets	
	7.11		Carried on as above.	
	8.11		ditto & improving drainage & raising bottoms of trenches	
	9.11		ditto	
	10.11		ditto	

WAR DIARY or INTELLIGENCE SUMMARY

Army Form C. 2118

1/97 Fd Co RE

page 2

Place	Date	Hour	Summary of Events and Information	Remarks and references to Appendices
Armentiers	11.11.15		Continued work on front line trenches 74 - 80	
	12.11		ditto also work in hand for two Batteries 97ᵃ Bde RFA	
			No 1 Sect returned from NERRIS	
	13.11		ditto No 1 commenced work on revetting 79 S with pors wire & needle	
	14.11		Work continued as on 13th. × on Artillery Observation Stations	
	15.		" " " " "	
	16		" " " " "	
	17		" " " " "	
	18		No 1 commenced to take over from No 4 Sect trenches 79 & 80	
	19		Work continued as above viz. No 2. 74 75 76 trenches	
			No 3. 77 78 "	
			No 1 79 80 "	
	20		No 4 Section commenced work under CRE on Camps & huts continuing work on Artillery Observation Stations Work continued as above.	

Army Form C. 2118

WAR DIARY of 97 Fd Co RE
or
INTELLIGENCE SUMMARY.

page 3

(Erase heading not required.)

Instructions regarding War Diaries and Intelligence Summaries are contained in F.S. Regs., Part II. and the Staff Manual respectively. Title pages will be prepared in manuscript.

Place	Date	Hour	Summary of Events and Information	Remarks and references to Appendices
Mentens	21.11.15		Work Continued as above.	
	22		ditto	
	23		ditto	
	24		ditto	
	25		ditto	
	26		ditto	
	27		ditto	
	28		ditto	
	29		ditto	
	30		ditto	
	31		ditto	
In support line			Summary of work done from 6.11.15 to 30.11.15	
			962 H continued parapet forwards revetment from revetment erected, also posts + hurdles wired together at traverses etc. Say 1000 run	
			61 Dugouts for 30 men each erected	
In support line Drainage			Revetting by posts wire netters. Drains cleared at 74 & 75 Trench.	

OSS???? MEMB???R.E.
O.G. 97th (FIELD) COY. R.E.

2353 Wt. W3544/1454 700,000 5/15 D.D.&I. A.D.S.S./Forms/C. 2118.

97 à FORC.
Vol: 4

Confidential

War Diary

of

97th Field Coy. Royal Engineers.

from 1st December 1915 to 31st December 1915.

(Volume 4).

Confidential

War Diary

of

97th Field Coy R.E.

From December 1st 1915 to December 31st 1915.

(Volume 4).

Secret-

WAR DIARY
INTELLIGENCE SUMMARY.

Army Form C. 2118.

9/ Fd Co. R.E
with 62 I.B. 21 Div

Place	Date	Hour	Summary of Events and Information — 74-80 Trenches at L'Epinette Sheet 36.N.W. 1.S.c.2.2 to C.28.c.3	Remarks and references to Appendices
Trenches	1.12.15		3 Section at work on revetting front line trenches 74-80. 1 Section at work on North line Centre's etc., and R.A. observing stations & gun emplacements.	
	2.12		ditto	
	3.12		ditto	
	4.12		ditto	
	5.12		ditto	
	6.12		Received information that 1st Northumbrian R.E. who had been at work on Communication trenches & concrete M.G. emplacements & dugout were leaving the Sector that day.	
	7.12		ditto	
	8.12		Continued work on Plank Av & Rond and Spain Av. water being above 18" dug in places, the trenches being no where revetted, and much fallen in.	
	9.12		Work on Plank Av raising walls boards to 6" above H.W.L. Plank Rd. Clearing falls & revetting Spain Av. removing duckboards and relaying on piles to a slope of two. Sappers engaged working on each fire trench	

Army Form C. 2118.

WAR DIARY
or
INTELLIGENCE SUMMARY.

(Erase heading not required.)

Instructions regarding War Diaries and Intelligence
Summaries are contained in F. S. Regs., Part II.
and the Staff Manual respectively. Title pages
will be prepared in manuscript.

Place	Date	Hour	Summary of Events and Information	Remarks and references to Appendices
	10.	12	Work Continued as on 9.12.16	
	11 to	12	ditto	
	24.	12	Holiday	
	25.	12	Commenced work on Strong points in 77 & 78	
	26.	12	ditto as on 9.12.16	
	27. 12 to		ditto	
	30. 12			

As regards the neighbourhood of trenches 74-80 — Experience shows that no trench with 4 feet of cover will stand unless revetted. Someday revetments should not be used for a breastwork higher than 3' 6".

6SSPludworth
Major R.E.
O.C. 97 Co. R.E
1.1.16

21st Divisional Engineers

97th FIELD COMPANY R. E. ::: JANUARY 1916.

Confidential

War Diary

of

97th Field Coy R.E.

from January 1st 1916 to January 31st 1916

(Volume 5).

Army Form C. 2118.

97th Field Coy R.E.

WAR DIARY
or
INTELLIGENCE SUMMARY.

(Erase heading not required.)

Instructions regarding War Diaries and Intelligence Summaries are contained in F. S. Regs., Part II. and the Staff Manual respectively. Title pages will be prepared in manuscript.

Place	Date	Hour	Summary of Events and Information	Remarks and references to Appendices
Armentières	1.1.15		No I Sec. Work on 79-80 trenches fire & support & Spain Av	
			No II Sec. " " 74-75-78 " " " — Plank Av & Plank R!	
			No III Sec. " " 79-78 " " " & Spain Av	
			No IV " in Armentières under CRE.	
	2		As above	
	3		" "	
	4		No 2 & 3 Sec finishes on Spain Av	
	5		As above	
	6		" "	
	7		" "	
	8		" "	
	9		No I - II - III Sec " " No 4 Sec starts work on Spain Av near Houplines	
	10		As above	
	11		No I Sec & 5 Sappers went on trestling out enterprise with R" NF ammunition as above	
	12		Do above for 10th	
	13		" "	
	14		" "	
	15		" "	

97th Field Coy, R.E. Army Form C. 2118.

WAR DIARY
or
INTELLIGENCE SUMMARY.
(Erase heading not required.)

Place	Date	Hour	Summary of Events and Information	Remarks and references to Appendices
Armentières	16/1/16		On Fr 15th No 4 Starts work on B intercom for from	
	17		As above	
	18		"	
	19		"	
	20		"	
	21		" No 3 Sec Starts work on SPY & SPZ	
	22		As above	
	23		"	
	24		"	
	25		"	
	27		"	
	28		"	
	29		"	
	30		"	
	31		"	

A.J. Martyn, E
Major, 97 Field Coy, R.E.

21st Divisional Engineers

97th FIELD COMPANY R. E. ::: FEBRUARY 1916.

Confidential.

War Diary

of

97th Field Coy R.E.

from 1st February to 29th February 1916.

(Volume 6.)

Army Form C. 2118.

WAR DIARY
or
INTELLIGENCE SUMMARY.   97 Fd Co RE
(Erase heading not required.)

1916

Instructions regarding War Diaries and Intelligence Summaries are contained in F. S. Regs., Part II. and the Staff Manual respectively. Title pages will be prepared in manuscript.

Place	Date	Hour	Summary of Events and Information	Remarks and references to Appendices
Armentières	1.2.16		The line being held by two Bdes in front line in place of three hitherto. 97 Co RE was moved to subsidiary line in town.	
	to		No 1 Sect Lille Post	
			No 2 " Town	
			No 3 " Subsidiary line between Australia Rd + River Lys.	
	11.2.16		No 4 " Continues on Buterne Farm	
	12.2.16		No 4 Section commences work on Buterne lane, remainder as above	
	13.2.16 to 29.2.16		ditto	

O.S. Humphreys Major RE
O.C. 97 Fd Co RE

21st Divisional Engineers

97th FIELD COMPANY R. E. ::: MARCH 1916.

Army Form C. 2118.

WAR DIARY
or
INTELLIGENCE SUMMARY.
(Erase heading not required.)

97th Fd Co RE

Place	Date	Hour	Summary of Events and Information	Remarks and references to Appendices
ARMENTIERES	1/3/16		No 1 Sec. Work on Lille Post.	
			No 2 " Work in town. Observation Posts, Horse lines etc.	
			No 3 " Work on Sub line & Com trenches. Nd of Australia Rd to R Lys behind Sub. line. Grazing & revetting trenches, building traverses & putting in dugouts.	
	2 – 10th		No 4 Sec Work on BUTERNE LANE. Grazing & revetting.	
	11th		Part of No 3 Sec starts revetting – grazing BUTERNE LANE	
			Other Secs as above.	
	11 – 19th		As above	
	20th		Part of No 3 Sec starts wiring in front of Houplines on the Cavalry Zin night work	
			No I Sec Lyft. Lille Post which was taken over by 77th Fd Co RE.	
	21st		No I Sec starts wiring in front of Houplines on the cavalry line Day work.	
			No 2 & No 4 as above.	
	22nd		No 2 Sec started wiring in front of Houplines on the cavalry line Day work.	
			Other sections as above.	
	23rd		The 78th Fd Co RE took over BUTERNE LANE.	
	24 "		No 4 Sec started wiring with the other sections.	
	25th		All sections wiring.	

WAR DIARY

INTELLIGENCE SUMMARY.

97th Fd Co. RE (continued)

Army Form C. 2118.

Place	Date	Hour	Summary of Events and Information	Remarks and references to Appendices
ARMENTIERES	26/3/18		All sections wiring in front of the cavalry line Houplines.	
	27 28 29		Coy wiring as above, shooting & grenade throwing	
	30	1 pm	Parade & march to BAILLEUL. Arrived there 5 pm & went into billets	
BAILLEUL	31	11.15 am	Parade & march to GODEWAERSVELDE. Arrived there 2 pm, entrained. Train left at 4.30 pm for LONGUEAU near AMIENS	

O.C. 97th Field Coy, R.E.

21st Divisional Engineers

97th FIELD COMPANY R. E. :::: A P R I L 1916.

Confidential

War Diary

of

97th Field Coy R.E.

from April 1st 1916 to April 30th 1916.

(Volume 8.)

Army Form C. 2118.

WAR DIARY

INTELLIGENCE SUMMARY

(Erase heading not required.)

97th Fd Co RE

Place	Date	Hour	Summary of Events and Information	Remarks and references to Appendices
LONGUEAU	1/4/16	3.30am	Arrived at LONGUEAU from GODEWAERSVELDE. Disentrained & marched to CARDONETTE arriving there at 10.30 am.	
CARDONNETTE	2nd–7th		Practiced shooting & erecting bridging materials. 7th No 3 Sec went to RIBEMONT for Div. HQ work.	
	8th		Paraded at 10.30 am & marched to BONNAY arriving at 2 pm.	
BONNAY	9th		Sunday.	
	10th		No 1 Sec w/r No 10 am for MEAULTE. No 4 Sec put the trestle across the river	
	11–12th		Starts working with for gun emplacements in AMIENS	
	13th		No 2 & 4 sections practiced putting trestles over the R. ANCRE.	
	14th		Occupied 7 No 2 section left at 9 am to go to the line to build huts near BECOURT-WOOD	
	15th		HQ & No 4 Sec works on building a shooting camp	
	16–17th		Occupied No 4 Sec repaired the Abri at BECOURT-WOOD. Remainder as above	
	18th	7.30am	Paraded & marched to VILLE. Arrived 10 am. No 4 Sec joined No 2 Sec at BECOURT WOOD.	
VILLE	19th		Coy HQ at VILLE. No 1 Sec in MEAULT. No 2 & 4 at BECOURT WOOD. No 3 at RIBEMONT. No 1, 2 & 4 secs employed on underground dugouts. No 3 making steel arch dugouts from rails.	
	23rd		No 3 Sec came to Ville & started work in the workshop erecting steel rail gun emplacements.	
	24th–3rd		As above.	

97th Field Coy RE

21st Divisional Engineers

97th FIELD COMPANY R. E. ::: M A Y 1 9 1 6

Confidential

War Diary
of
97th Field Coy R.E.

from May 1st 1916   to   May 31st 1916.

(Volume 9.)

Army Form C. 2118.

WAR DIARY
or
INTELLIGENCE SUMMARY.
(Erase heading not required.)

94th Field Coy R.E.

Place	Date	Hour	Summary of Events and Information	Remarks and references to Appendices
VILLE	1/5/16		No I Sec. Work on Iridon Dugout 6pm at	
			No II Sec. Work on Iridon Dugout.	
			No III Sec. Work on Sawmill building & artillery emplacements &c	
		3ᵃ.5	No IV Sec. Work on Dugout.	
			No I Sec. un-drilled ad 9 thier billet – moved to sap 7 MOLANCOURT - MEAULTE Rd	
			Remainder a chan.	
		6ᵃ.5	Band raw flanks workin	
		14"	Circular raw flanks workin. No I Sec. moved to hut at BECOURT VALLEY	
			No I - II - IV Sec. work on revetting trenches – Dugout – gun emplacements &c.	
			No 3 m a chm	
	31"			

21st Divisional Engineers

97th FIELD COMPANY R. E. ::: JUNE 1916.

War Diary
of
97th Field Coy R.E.
from June 1st 1916 to June 30th 1916.
(Volume 10).

Army Form C. 2118.

WAR DIARY
or
INTELLIGENCE SUMMARY.

(Erase heading not required.)

94th Field Coy R.E.

Place	Date	Hour	Summary of Events and Information	Remarks and references to Appendices
VILLE	1/6/16		No 1 Sec. Work on Dressing Station KINGS.AV.	
	2/6		Dug out BECOURT. Reclaiming WILLOW AV. Ammn stores in TANGIER	
	3/6		O.P's for artillery.	
	4/6		Saw mill, gun emplacements in Grand VILLE	
	5/6		Dug outs BECOURT. Heavy T.M. emplacement, Traversing RONDEL NEW AV.	
			LT SPARKS leaves 63 Inf Bde H.Qrs	
			No 3 Sec. to BECOURT & joins No 2 Section for work in Grand VILLE	
	6/6		Work on TAMBOUR. KINGS. AV. WILLOW AV. & ARTILLERY O.P.	
			Lt Clarke joined this unit & went to BECOURT	
			No 4 SEC. T 1 Co ?AY & L. Supervised Recesses in trenches. Dr. gas contracted Bg	
	20		Lt Collyns. rejoined this unit from Base	
	20		Lt Col Clark to hospital with [illeg] Tonsilitis	
	21		2 stells in yard killing 2 horses & severely wounding another	
	23		Overhead Tramway Completed 700 x ABERDEEN AV. for H.T.M.B amm T gun.	
	24		Lt Rouse & No 4 Section drive VILLE From BECOURT VALLEY.	
	25		Holiday at Ville. LT NESTOR & No I Section arrive VILLE from BECOURT VALLEY	
	26		Shell (13cm) burst in billet killed 11 Died of Wounds 3 Other wounded 6 O.R.	
			MV home Lt W. Warsden Lt RH Gillespie Lt Pa LtE Plastow Wounded.	
	27		Lt Clarke rejoined	
	28		No 3 Sec repaired water pipe on KINGSTON TRENCH	
	29		Lts McLEAN McDONALD & HORNBY 227 N 18 O.R. joined at VILLE	
	30		No 3 sec repaired overhead rly. + H.T.M.B. emplacement at BON ACCORD	
	31		Lts CLARKE & HORNBY 2 O.R. Nos 1 & 4 Section moved to Assembly Trenches MARESCHAL ST.	
			Rem of Coy moved 700,000 5/15 D.D.&L M c PHERSON 14 N.F. at MEAVITE at 8 pm.	

CHAPMAN O.C. 94th Field Coy R.E.

Army Form C. 2118.

WAR DIARY
or
INTELLIGENCE SUMMARY.

(Erase heading not required.)

97th Field Coy R.E.

Place	Date	Hour	Summary of Events and Information	Remarks and references to Appendices
VILLE	JUNE 1916		During APRIL MAY & JUNE There was considerable shortage of Timber from abroad for CORPS. A portable Band Saw for breaking down logs was erected at VILLE and working on MAY 7th. Later other machines were erected as required, including a 36" Circular saw, Small circular saw, Drilling machine & "later a Saw sharpening machine. Forges, hammer & power driven blowing fan etc. The whole worked by portable engine Ruston & W.D. oil engine, with a requisitioned portable engine as spare.	

[signature]

MAJOR. R.E.,
O.C. 97th (FIELD) COY. R.E.

21st Divisional Engineers

97th FIELD COMPANY R. E. ::: JULY 1916.

CONFIDENTIAL

WAR DIARY.

OF

97th FIELD Co. R.E.

JULY, 1916.

Army Form C. 2118.

WAR DIARY
or
INTELLIGENCE SUMMARY.
(Erase heading not required)

July 1916 9th (Field) Cy R.E. 21st Dn

Place	Date	Hour	Summary of Events and Information	Remarks and references to Appendices
BECOURT VALLEY	July 1st	7.32 am	Nos 1 & 4 Sections went over parapet and worked in that neighbourhood till they were relieved. No 4 Section reached BIRCH TREE WOOD but had to retire to SUNKEN RD where they worked until they were relieved. No 1 Section reached LOZENGE TRENCH	
		7.30 am	No 2 Section marched from VILLE SUR L'ANCRE to BECOURT VALLEY.	
		12.30 pm	2/Lt R.A. COLLINS rejoins.	
		11pm	Nos 2 & 3 Sections with two Sections 98th R.E. dug trench across NO MAN'S LAND at GUILDFORD facing FRICOURT.	
			Total Casualties during the day. 2/Lt J.H. HORNBY wounded 29 O.R., all of Nos 1 & 4 Section. Killed wounded & missing.	

Army Form C. 2118.

WAR DIARY
or
INTELLIGENCE SUMMARY.
(Erase heading not required.)

Place	Date	Hour	Summary of Events and Information	Remarks and references to Appendices
BECOURT VALLEY	July 2nd	2am	No 1 Section received orders to return to BECOURT VALLEY.	
		11am	No 4 " " " " " "	
		8am	Nos 2 & 3 Sections 97th R.E. with 2 sections 98th R.E. & Pioneers marched off from old No Man's Land at GUILDFORD, alongside from FRICOURT being at our end, Lt HOWORTH reporting by telephone to this effect through Capt DAVIS MT.M. 21 DIV. Patrol of 97th R.E. proceeded to FRICOURT via German Support trench. Reports sent to C.R.E. & 21 DIV that FRICOURT VILLAGE, WOOD, & FARM probably evacuated by enemy at 9.15 & 9.30 am.	
	3	2pm	Nos 1 & 3 Sections bridge trenches from Kings Cross to Sunken Rd.	
		4pm	Whole company to BIRCH TREE & SHELTER WOODS to make strong points. Lt Y. LOWE rejoins.	
	4	1am	Company leaves strong points & returns to BECOURT VALLEY at 3am, according to orders received.	
		7am	Company leaves BECOURT VALLEY marches to DERNANCOURT & entrain. Transport marches to ARGOEUVRES.	

Army Form C. 2118.

WAR DIARY
or
INTELLIGENCE SUMMARY.
(Erase heading not required.)

Instructions regarding War Diaries and Intelligence Summaries are contained in F.S. Regs., Part II. and the Staff Manual respectively. Title pages will be prepared in manuscript.

Place	Date	Hour	Summary of Events and Information	Remarks and references to Appendices
BECOURT	July 4 & 5		Coy remounted men marched to DERNANCOURT & entrained for ARGOEUVRES. Transport marched from VILLE to ARGOEUVRES.	
ARGOEUVRES	6		rest. reinforcement 17. O.R.	
"	7		Coy marched to SAISSEVAL.	
SAISSEVAL	8		Rest	
"	9	6.30 p	Transport marched to QUERRIEU.	
"	10		Remainder men moved by train to CORBIE & marched to bivouac west of VILLE.	
VILLE	11		Dismounted men marched to BECOURT VALLEY. Transport to MEAULTE.	
BECOURT VALLEY	12		97 RE & 1 Co 14 NF ordered to march off at 4 PM to work on Tramway north from Bottom Wood	
	13		Continued work on Tramway, repaired to QUADRANGLE SUPPORT TRENCH at 11 PM say 1500 yds	
	14		Whole company ordered to bivouac south edge of FRICOURT WOOD. R/[...] moved	
South of FRICOURT WOOD	15		Made strong points in BAZENTIN LE PETIT WOOD. Position factory point no 11 occupied by enemy reinforcements. O.R. 29.	
"	16		Rest day.	
	17	7.30 pm	Lt HOWORTH & mix with to BAZENTIN-LE-PETIT WOOD to site strong point no 11 & with push pipes to prepare for blowing up enemy strong point 60x in front. Enemy were still in position & party were unable to work. Casualty. Wounded O.R. 1.	
			Work on strong points in BAZENTIN-LE-PETIT WOOD continued. Reconnaissance by 97 O.R.E. at 8.45 PM proved that enemy had vacated north edge of wood & their posts to north of support & [...] to that effect at 9.45 PM. Work on S.P. no 11 & Sunken Road commenced.	
"	18	10 am	Coy marched to BILLETS at BUIRE.	
BUIRE	19	4 pm	Coy marched to ALLONVILLE. reinforcements 13. O.R.	

Army Form C. 2118.

WAR DIARY
or
INTELLIGENCE SUMMARY.

(Erase heading not required.)

Instructions regarding War Diaries and Intelligence Summaries are contained in F. S. Regs., Part II. and the Staff Manual respectively. Title pages will be prepared in manuscript.

Place	Date	Hour	Summary of Events and Information	Remarks and references to Appendices
ALLONVILLE	July 20		rest.	
"	21		"	
"	22	2.30p	Coy marched to LONGEAU.	
		10.10p	entrained & left for ST POL	
ST POL	23	5am	arrived, marched to billets TERNAS. reinforcement. O.R. one.	
TERNAS	24	4pm	marched to GIVENCHY - LE - NOBLE	
GIVENCHY LE-NOBLE	25		rest	
"	26		"	
"	27			
"	28	1pm	Coy moved to ARRAS. motor lorries.	
ARRAS	29	2.30p	transport marched to MONTENESCOURT.	
	30		Officers & NCO's visit trenches - J Sector just north of R. Scarpe. No 3 Section trench tramway. No 1, 2, & 4 deep dug out in support line	
	31		ditto	

B.S. Plumpton E May 04 E
2.8.16 O.C. 4/Fd Co R E

21st Divisional Engineers

97th FIELD COMPANY R. E. ::: AUGUST 1916.

Army Form C. 2118.

Vol 12

AUGUST.

WAR DIARY
or
INTELLIGENCE SUMMARY.

(Erase heading not required.)

Place	Date	Hour	Summary of Events and Information	Remarks and references to Appendices
ARRAS	1.8.		97 F.D. CO. R.E.	
			No 1 Section commence work on dugout in FEBRUARY AV.	
			No 2 " " " " 2 dugouts in 86 & 92 SUPPORTS	
			No 3 " " " " on French Tramway OCTOBER AV.	
			No 4 " " " " dugouts No 41, 42, 43, 44, 45 & 46 in SUPPORT LINE	
	2.8.		ditto	
	3.8.		"	
	4.8.		"	
	5.8.		"	
	6.8.		No 1 Section commence machine gun emplacement	
	7.8.		ditto	
	8.8.		"	
	9.8.		"	
	10.8.		" No 4 Section holiday	
	11.8.		"	
	12.8.		No 4 Commence dugout No 47 BOSKY RDT.	
			No 3 Commence artillery O.P. at ST SAUVEUR	
	13.8.		"	
	14.8.		"	
	15.8.		"	
	16.8.		No 1 Section Holiday	
	17.8.		No 2 " " Holiday	
	18.8.		No 2 commenced cookhouse – JULY AV. and also DIVISIONAL BATHS.	
	19.8.		"	
	20.8.		No 1 stopped work on M.G. EMPLACEMENT.	

Army Form C. 2118.

WAR DIARY
or
INTELLIGENCE SUMMARY.
(Erase heading not required.)

97 F.D Co R.E

Place	Date	Hour	Summary of Events and Information	Remarks and references to Appendices
ARRAS	21.8		No 1 Section commence drawing FEBRUARY AV. No 4 Cookhouse BOSKY RDT.	
	22.8			
	23.8		No 1 commence dugout in 8Y track	
			No 3 commence brick telephone dugout ST. NICHOLAS	
	24.8		No 4 work on NICOLLS RDT.	
	25.8		No 2 commence drawing JULY AV.	
	26.8		No 3 commence emplacement for 60lb T.M. in FEBRUARY AV	
	27.8		No 3 & 4 sections holiday	
	28.8		No 1 T.2	
	29.8		No 3 complete telephone dugout. No 1 section 1 man wounded	
	30.8			
	31.8			

O.C. 97 F.D.Co R.E

21st Divisional Engineers

97th FIELD COMPANY R. E. ::: SEPTEMBER 1916.

Vol 13

War Diary
of
97th Field Coy R.E.

from September 1st 1916 to September 30th 1916.
(Volume 13).

1.10.16.

WFisher Capt R.E.
O.C. 97th (FIELD) COY. R.E.

Army Form C. 2118.

WAR DIARY
or
INTELLIGENCE SUMMARY.
(Erase heading not required.)

97th Field Cy RE

Place	Date SEPT	Hour	Summary of Events and Information	Remarks and references to Appendices
ARRAS	1		No1 Section working on dugout in 87 French	
	2	"	" draining JULY AVENUE	
	3	"	" emptying on emplacement for medium T·M in FEBRUARY AVENUE	
	4	"	" working NICHOLL'S REDOUBT.	
			Same	
			Same	
		1-0 pm	Section cleaning billets	
		1-30 pm	No1 Section left ARRAS	
		2-0 "	No 2 " " "	Marched to NOYELLETTE
		2-30 "	3 " " "	
		2-30 "	4 " " "	
		2-30	H.Q. & Transport marched from DUISANS to NOYELLETTE	
		5-30	Section wagons marched to NOYELLETTE	
NOYELLETTE	5	10-am	Company marched to SOMBRIN	
SOMBRIN	6		Company training	
	7		" "	
	8		" "	
	9		" "	
	10		" "	
	11		" " Received Div O.O. 67	
	12	9-30 am	Company marched to RUTHIE to billets	
RUTHIE	13	9-15 am	Marched to BERNANCOURT	
BERNANCOURT	14		Remained at BERNANCOURT. Received G.2.1.5. O.O. 91. at midnight	
	15	9-400	Marched to BECORDEL CAMP	
BECORDEL CAMP	16	9·00 am	Marched to POMMIERS REDOUBT	
	17	4 pm	Marched to BIVOUACS 500 yards NORTH OF BERNAFAY WOOD	
NORTH of BERNAFAY WOOD	17	1 pm	Four section 97 & two sections 126 CRE communicated with a three strong points. Approximate positions SP.1. T.2. B.1.6.; SP.2. N.32. C.4.1.; SP.3. N.31. d. 3.2 .. GAS ALLEY just in front of S.P.1 was already blocked against reported enemy bombers but information was received that GAS ALLEY near BULLS ROAD was again held by us. At 9.30 pm there was no one in CAP TRENCH	

Army Form C. 2118.

WAR DIARY
or
INTELLIGENCE SUMMARY.
(Erase heading not required.)

97th Field Cy R.E.

Place	Date	Hour	Summary of Events and Information	Remarks and references to Appendices
NORTH OF BERNAFAY WOOD	SEPT 17		Contact with division on right doubtful	
		1:45 am	Working party of 1st Lines put to work on extending S.P.2 towards W.N.W. No trace of an working party to both on SUPPORT-ASSEMBLY trench. A fine narrow trench join S.P.1 to Bn HQs. Work near front interrupted by enemy fire. BARRAGE on FLERS ROAD astride at 7 pm making at 8pm. Dustboards much needed on FLERS ROAD and from points 81 to FLERS. AVENUE. COCOA LANE impracticable at night when day. FLERS AVENUE much shelled. Have formed dump of RE stores at point 81 wire pickets sandbags. Cavalier 1 O.R. slightly wounded H.E.	
	18	4 pm	MAJOR B's PHILPOTTS left to go to 38th DIV as C.R.E.	
		7:30 pm	4 section 97 & 2 section 126 continued work on strong pt. No 3 & 2 completed gird entanglement. No 2 no wire. No infantry holding these points. communication between S.P.1 and division on night not made.	
	19	8 pm	2 section dug trench survey east of S.P.1 but did not get into touch with 20 Y division on right.	
	20	6 pm	2 section under CAPT SHAKESPEARE worked on cleaning FLERS-LONGUEVAL Road.	
	21	6 pm	2 section 97 RE with 60 infantry finished trench. above, & connected with 20 division on right made 200 overmen loads of pickets & wire and dumped them on FLERS. LONGUEVAL road two sections carried 60 oui man loads of pickets & wire to SUNKEN ROAD about 200 yds south of BULLS ROAD	
		10.40 pm	received C.R.E. O.O. No 3.	
	22	6.30 pm	CAPT J.T. FISHER joined the company & took command	
		6 pm	2 section made good GAS ALLEY from SWITCH TRENCH to CAP TRENCH. 500 yds 1 section with 120 infantry cleared FLERS-LONGUEVAL Road from edge of DELVILLE ROAD for 300 yds north	
	23	8.0 am	1 section carrying material to DV DUMP south of LONGUEVAL	
		6-0 pm	2 sections carried 60 man loads of pickets & wire to forward dump N.32.C.53	
		10.20 pm	C.R.E. O.O. No 3 received	
		11.30 pm	1 section with two companies infantry working on FLERS-LONGUEVAL road.	
	24	7.0 am	1 section in L morning with 2 Cn Infantry & laid a trumline 60 cm from la GRANDE PLACE	
		10 pm	3 - - in afternoon - 2 Cn PUNJAUB LONGUEVAL to 15 C" to put the road junction at	
			Mr S W Corner of DELVILLE WOOD Casualties in morning 5 killed & 7 wounded 1 slightly	

Army Form C. 2118.

WAR DIARY
or
INTELLIGENCE SUMMARY.

(Erase heading not required.)

94th Field Coy RE.

Instructions regarding War Diaries and Intelligence Summaries are contained in F.S. Regs., Part II. and the Staff Manual respectively. Title pages will be prepared in manuscript.

Place	Date	Hour	Summary of Events and Information	Remarks and references to Appendices
BERNAFAY WOOD	26	12.30pm	Laid Decauville track to a point 250ˣ from the edge of DELVILLE Wood finished 5pm (2 sections)	
		6.30pm	Marched out & 1 Platoon proceeded to a front road N27 a 6.0 & put what were 2 sections C in front of 2 machine guns & across the road also dug a trench across the road and for about 20 yds to the side of it, average depth 3'6" arrived in camp 3:30 am 27th	
	27		Other section taken up from a dump at N32 b 4.3.	
		7:30 am	2 Sections were laying Decauville tramway from crossroads at S17 a 4.2 to the crossroads in LONGUEVAL & completing it on the other side of LONGUEVAL to S18 b 10.0	
		4:30pm	Clearing the road through FLERS & making it fit for two transport lately by	
		6:30pm	2 Platoons of Pioneers	
		7:30pm		
	28	7:30am	2 Sections completed the tramway	
		[illegible] 5:30pm	2 sections + 1 Coy Pioneers to clearing road from road junction in FLERS to cross-roads S of GUEUDECOURT & making an R.E. Dump etc in cutting	
		6:30am		
		8:0am	2 sections S of FLERS also filling a trench which ran from the at NE corner of FLERS also filling a trench which ran from S of FLERS which were taken over by another section	

WAR DIARY
INTELLIGENCE SUMMARY

94th Field Coy RE. Army Form C. 2118.

Place	Date	Hour	Summary of Events and Information	Remarks and references to Appendices
N of BERNA-FAY Wood	29/9/16	6:30am	1 Section repaired the Decauville track along the S edge of DELVILLE wood & section tram bridges in MONTAUBAN & made light trench bridges for the FLERS — GUEDECOURT Road	
		2:0 pm		
		8:30 pm	1 Section with 1 Coy Infantry cleared the road between LONGUEVAL and FLERS and laid bricks. 1 Section + 1 Coy Infantry took scissor pickets & bridges up to N 31 b 0.3 and laid on across the first trench at N 31 b 5.3. They were exhibited. The R.E. Stores into 1 dump at N 31 b 0.3 and the cleared & filled holes in the road through FLERS	
	30/9/16	9:0 am	2 sections laid bricks and repaired the road working N from LONGUEVAL. They also mended 2 breaks in the tramway	
		8:30 pm	1 section + 1 Coy Pioneer went to FLERS with scissor pickets but the N N of the village was of 17 mm being heavily shelled so that they worked on the S end after about 1 hour the party attached with the scissor pickets for the dump but 7 were wounded before they got more than about 200x so they left the pickets east of N 31 c 3.5 and worked on the road 1 section and 2 Coy Infantry dug dump below on the the road between FLERS + LONGUEVAL	Major Luft RE OC 94 Fd Coy RE

21st Divisional Engineers

97th FIELD COMPANY R. E. ::: OCTOBER 1916.

OCTOBER

Army Form C. 2118.

WAR DIARY or INTELLIGENCE SUMMARY.

97th Field Coy. RE Vol 14

(Erase heading not required.)

Place	Date	Hour	Summary of Events and Information	Remarks and references to Appendices
N of BERNA- FAY WOOD	2/10/16	8.0 a.m	Marched to BUIRE & Entrained there under canvas arriving 1 h.m.	
	3/10/16	12.10 p.m	Transport marched to ARGOEUVRES arriving 10.0 p.m & were billeted	
	4/10/16	10.0 a.m	Company marched to RIBEMONT entrained 12.30 p.m arrived LONGPRÉ 4.30 p.m detrained & marched to BUCHON arriving 6.0 p.m & were billeted.	
			Transport left ARGOEUVRES 10.0 a.m & reached BUCHON at 5.30 p.m	
	5/10/16		Rested & overhauled equipment	
	6/10/16		ditto	
	7/10/16		ditto	
	8/10/16	9.0 a.m	Marched to LONG PRÉ entrained at 1.0 p.m left at 4.15 p.m arrived at FOUQUEREUIL 4.30 a.m marched to MARLES LES MINES arriving 7.30 a.m rested	
	10/10/16		Rested 10.0 a.m left for NOYELLES LES VERMELLES and took over billets & work from 151st C.R.E.	
	11/10/16		from 151st C.R.E. arriving there at 3.0 p.m	

WAR DIARY
INTELLIGENCE SUMMARY

91st Field Coy, R.E.

Army Form C. 2118.

Place	Date	Hour	Summary of Events and Information	Remarks and references to Appendices
NOYELLES LES VERMELLES	12/10/16		Work on dugouts in the QUARRIES SECTOR. 1 section hard worker & refinement	
	13/10/16		ditto but each section had 50 infantry attached	
	14/10/16		ditto	
	15/10/16		Both 4 diving billets. Infantry working parties working & eighteen shelters for Vickers was	
	16/10/16		Work as dugouts continued	
	17/10/16		"	
	18/10/16		"	
	19/10/16		"	
	20/10/16		"	
	21/10/16		Infantry with drawn. work resumed in willing parties	
	22/10/16		Both	
	23/10/16		Commenced work on something for hurdles supplied to reserve line. also continued	
	24/10/16		with 7 dug outs work commenced on defensive programme extra work	
	25/10/16		to attached	

Army Form C. 2118.

WAR DIARY
or
INTELLIGENCE SUMMARY.
(Erase heading not required.)

97th Field Coy R.E.

Place	Date	Hour	Summary of Events and Information	Remarks and references to Appendices
NOYELLES LES VERMELLES	Nov 26th 27th		Work continued	
	28th 29th		Baths	
	30th		Rabbit Run revetted 80' from North end	
	31st		Highland Trench - 30' in centre (Working parties of available 90 - 3 days) 6 Frames fixed in Dug out in HIGHLAND TRENCH CROWN TRENCH. 16 claws in the Shafts cut in Dug out in NEW LAVEER Lane. 70' of Revement revetted at various spots 40' of Trench laid and boarded 2 Dug outs for New Battalion H.Q. finished 1 in Support line finished except for bracing & side shuting a new one commenced at Old Bd H.Q & a 3rd one at New Bd H.Q Dug out in Chapel ALLEY 10 frames fixed	

Mis Dun Engh MA

O.C. 97th Fd Coy RE

Copy.

62nd Infantry Brigade
Approximate Programme of Work for 97th Field Coy. R.E.

No: 1 section and 40 men from Reserve Bn.
RABBIT RUN, to be revetted at night
DRUMMOND & HIGHLAND TRENCH
Also to make beds & fix stoves in dugouts & shelters for Left Coy & Support Coy of Left Bn.

No: 2 section and 60 men from Support Bn.
Dugout, NEW LANCER LANE.
Dugout, CROWN TRENCH.
Dugout, HIGHLAND TRENCH.
Also beds for Centre & right Coy of Left Bn.

No: 3 section and 100 men from Support Bn.
Revetting & grading Reserve Line commencing from junction of GORDON ALLEY and O.B.1, working both ways.
Repairing tramway to O.B.5
Beds & stoves for Right Bn.
Also lend 6 men to Div. Art. for T.M. emplacement

No: 4 section and 66 men from Support Bn.
Complete Dugout, CHAPEL ALLEY.
"   "   in Support Line between BOYAU 78 and 77a.
2 Dugouts at Bn. Hd. Qrs.
Beds and stoves for Right Bn.

Each Group will have an R.E. Officer to advise.
Tomorrow 23rd, No: 1 section Officer will report at 1st Lincoln R. Hd. Qrs. and remaining R.E. Officers at 13th N.F. Hd. Qrs. to arrange reliefs, etc.
The above working parties will parade at 10. a.m in the most convenient trench in the direction of their new work area.
They will then be told off.

22/7/16

(sd) R.C. Hobson 2nd Lt
Acting Bde Major

21st Divisional Engineers

97th FIELD COMPANY R. E. ::: NOVEMBER 1916.

CONFIDENTIAL

WAR DIARY

of

97th Field Co R.E.

FROM 1st Novr 1916 to 30th Novr 1916

Army Form C. 2118.

WAR DIARY
or
INTELLIGENCE SUMMARY.
(Erase heading not required.)

Instructions regarding War Diaries and Intelligence
Summaries are contained in F.S. Regs., Part II.
and the Staff Manual respectively. Title pages
will be prepared in manuscript.

Place	Date	Hour	Summary of Events and Information	Remarks and references to Appendices
NOYELLES Les VERMELLES	1/11/16		Went entrained on dug outs & water	
	4/11/16		The pumps were started in Noyelles Vermelles & 1 well emerged to hut quarters water from interior. 1 pump at O.B.4 repaired & water found suitable for drinking. Brigade Baths fitted up in VERMELLES	
	5/11/16		Baths & Wells inspection	
	6/11/16		Same work continued Dug outs at BOYAU 78 CHAPEL ALLEY & the 3rd Dug out at the reservoir in Béthune H.Q. completed remainder left for a much a N than the well was started & is in clay but water construction in HIGHLAND TRENCH and water found 7 ft below the floor but owing to hard chalk great difficulty is being experienced in driving it 2/h Wiring N.E. gallery started constructing new dug outs	
	11/11/16		in the area concerning work started in a new programme Turning to 1200 mod Work started in working on STANSFIELD R?	
	12/11/16		Baths & filling gas blankets	

WAR DIARY
or
INTELLIGENCE SUMMARY.

Army Form C. 2118.

Place	Date	Hour	Summary of Events and Information	Remarks and references to Appendices
NOYELLES LES VERMELLES	13/4/16		Work on & new programme writing trenches & training	
	18/4/16		Baths & trench inspection	
	24/4/16		Work on new programme also (range) the wokmen from the met mine (1000 x)	
	25/4/16		on 3 miles/hr & blowing HULLUCH, GORDON ALLEY, DEVON LANE 0.3.1. (mines) held up by bad weather SACKVILLE St also 200 ft of Front line South of BRECON SAP & Trenching job for horse trophe for 1500 x Another explode so far as 0.3.1 Baths etc	
	26/4/16			
	27/4/16		Ruling continued HULLUCH ALLEY widened & reverted CHAPEL ALLEY complete to 0.9.1 + hudin commencing on the support line	
	30/4/16			

Additional Work Programme.

Two R.E's will report daily at 9. a.m. at each Coy. H.Q. of the battalions in the Front and Immediate Support Line, Sundays excepted.

10 Men at least per Company, and as many more as possible will be there at the same time to-morrow Nov. 11th, but on the following days will start work independently at 8.30 a.m.

The above parties with work will consist of repairing and revetting the front line, the immediate support line and the beyans joining these two lines.

Support Battn. supplies 160 men a day to repair communication Trenches in advance of O.B.4 (less Hulluch and Gordon Alleys) and also that part of the Reserve line which lies in advance of O.B.1.

    30 men meet R.E's at junction of St. George's Trench and Dudley Lane at 9. a.m.

    30 men meet R.E's at junction of O.G.1 and Devon Lane at 9 a.m.

    30 men at 9 a.m. in Chapel Alley back to junction with O.B.1.

    30 men at 9 a.m. on Chapel Alley from O.B.1. to O.B.4. Meet R.E's at junction of Chapel Alley and O.B.4.

    40 men on O.G.1 north of Devon Lane. Meet at 9. a.m. at junction of Fosse Way and O.G.1.

Reserve Battalion will work on O.B.4., O.B.5 and Curly Crescent and the Communication Trenches between those lines. Party to meet R.E. at Bde H.Q. at 9. a.m. daily.

20 men of 13 North'd Fus. quartered in Vermelles will work nightly on Railway. They will meet R.E's at Mansion House at 9. p.m.

20 men from 13th North'd Fus., Vermelles party, and 40 men from 12 North'd Fus., Vermelles party, work on O.B.1, and meet R.E's at Mansion House daily at 8.30 a.m.

40 men of 1 Lincoln R. from Vermelles work daily on Hulluch Alley and Gordon Alley. This party will meet R.E's at Mansion House at 8.30 a.m.

Machine Gunners and half Pioneers work on Village

Line and Chapel Alley to Vermelles, and all Communication Trenches from Curly Crescent backwards. A few of these Pioneers will be detailed to repair all trench boards in every Communication Trench.

Half Pioneers continue on DugOuts in Devon Lane and Stonefield Road

Reserve Battn. 10 extra men daily to carry for L.T.M. Bty 9 a.m. junction of Fosse Way and Curly Crescent.

Reserve Battn 40 men to meet R.E's at junction O.B. 4. and Gordon Alley at 9 a.m. for work on T Heads in Gordon Alley.

Support Bn. 40 men to clean T. Heads. in Devon Lane and dig new Shelters on opposite side.

All spare men to work on the Trenches in immediate vicinity of their dwellings, and Machine Gunners to put T. heads in Chapel Alley in good condition

(Sd) H.R. Gallatly
Capt.
Bde. Major
62 Infantry Brigade

10th Nov. 1916.

62 Brigade
B.M. 598
Nov. 1916.

21st Divisional Engineers

97th FIELD COMPANY R. E. ::: DECEMBER 1916.

Vol 16

War Diary
of
97th Field Coy R.E.
for
December 1st 1916 to December 31st 1916.
(Volume 16.)

Army Form C. 2118.

WAR DIARY
or
INTELLIGENCE SUMMARY.
(Erase heading not required.)

97th Field Coy R.E.

Place	Date	Hour	Summary of Events and Information	Remarks and references to Appendices
NOYELLES LES VERMELLES	1/12/16		Work continued on trenches and tramways. O.P. in VERMELLES for B.94.RFA commenced	
	2.12.16		GORDON ALLEY cleared for third time after damage by hostile T.M.s.	
	3.12.		Baths and inspection.	
	4.12 to 6.12		Work as above. Much work caused by hostile bombardment of trenches with shells & mortars	
	9.12		A door fixed in NEWPORT CRATER. Shelters constructed in STANSFIELD ROAD, Elephant shelters erected in DEVON LANE and O.G.1. Commenced dugout in CHAPEL ALLEY for T.M.B.	
	6/12		O.P. in VERMELLES sustained a direct hit from 5.9 gun and was completely destroyed - no casualties.	
	8/12		LT. W.W. MARSDEN rejoined from ENGLAND	
	10/12		Baths and inspection. 11 LT. G. G. MACLEAN returned from leave.	
	11/12 to 16/12		Work as for last week. Many falls in trenches caused by wet weather. Work on dugout for Z/21 TMB continued. Commenced to make down for infantry communication to front line. Shelters erected in DEVON LANE. Ballasting tramway reached CURLY CRESCENT. Roof of dressing station in O.G.1 covered with felt. Ammunition store improved for C/94 R.F.A. & tramway of water pipe (1½") along DEVON LANE commenced. Commenced new dugout for signals at Bde H.Qs. & improved roof of Bde Major's dugout.	
	13/12		CAPT. J.T.FISHER on LEAVE.	
	15.12		LT. G.E. HOWORTH. returned from Div. SCHOOL and appointed ADJUTANT. CRE. 21 D.W.	
	18/12 to 23.12		Work continued on trenches. Hostile shell & T.M. fire very heavy. Much damage caused to trenches	
	22.12./ 23.12.		Officers & NCOs of 1/2 West Riding Fd Coy RE(T) were taken round the trenches & the work handed over to them	
	24.12		Baths. Cleaning equipment & Weekly Inspection	

Army Form C. 2118.

WAR DIARY
or
INTELLIGENCE SUMMARY.

(Erase heading not required.)

Instructions regarding War Diaries and Intelligence Summaries are contained in F. S. Regs., Part II. and the Staff Manual respectively. Title pages will be prepared in manuscript.

Place	Date	Hour	Summary of Events and Information	Remarks and references to Appendices
NOVELLES LES MINES	25.12		Christmas Day.	
MERMELLES	26.12	9.10 am	Marched to MARLES LES MINES. Arrived 2.30 pm. billets	
MARLES LES MINES	27.12		Cleaned billets. Clothes, equipment	
	28.12		Erected hut for ADMS at LABEUVRIERE.	
	29.12		Baths & Drill	
	30.12		Drill & improving horse standings & parade ground.	
	31.12		Church Parade	

CONFIDENTIAL.

Vol 17

WAR DIARY.

OF

97th (Field) Co. R.E.

FROM   JAN. 1. 1917
TO   JAN. 31. 1917.

CONFIDENTIAL.

Army Form C. 2118.

WAR DIARY
INTELLIGENCE SUMMARY.
(Erase heading not required.)

97th Field Coy R.E

Place	Date	Hour	Summary of Events and Information	Remarks and references to Appendices
MARLES	1/1/17		Training tent	
LES	2/1/17		1 Section to MAZINGARBE by two lorries / horsed wagon also	
MINES			Capt FISHER to R.E. School LE PARC	
	3/1/17		2d MARSDEN to be acting adjutant to C.R.E. 21st Div	
	4/1/17		Training tent	
	10/1/17		Capt FISHER returned	
	11/1/17		2d MARSDEN appointed captain in 126th & R.E.	
	12/1/17		Training tent	
	20/1/17		No1 Section returned having done the following	
	20/1/17		Cleared drained & repaired the reserve line from HAY ALLEY to DEVON Lane	

WAR DIARY
INTELLIGENCE SUMMARY

Army Form C. 2118.

9 M Field Coy R.E.

Place	Date	Hour	Summary of Events and Information	Remarks and references to Appendices
	25/1/17		H.Q. M.G. Made an M.G. emplacement in B field hut at junction of Devon Lane & the reserve line	
	26/1/17		Put up a gun turning obstacle in reserve trench 100 yards to left of DEVON Lane	
	27/1/17		Training & rest	
	28/1/17		Transport by road & Sappers by rail via CHOCQUES & POPERINGHE, detrained 3 miles ENE of POPERINGHE. Transport arrived 1 night at NEUF BERQUIN. A short march to Sappers' Transport arrived 7.30 pm	
	29/1/17		A march from rest into reconnoitred R.E. supplies & Reserve line to north so far as OOSTVLETEREM reminder fixed up hosepipe line	
	30/1/17		Commenced wiring belts	
	31/1/17		1 section Hutting in camp. 1 section on defence of ELVERDINGHE. 2 sections on standing lines SW ELVERDINGHE	

CONFIDENTIAL

Vol 18

WAR DIARY

OF

97th Field Co. R.E.

21st Division

1st – 28th Feb 1917.

Army Form C. 2118.

WAR DIARY
or
INTELLIGENCE SUMMARY.

(Erase heading not required.)

Instructions regarding War Diaries and Intelligence Summaries are contained in F. S. Regs., Part II. and the Staff Manual respectively. Title pages will be prepared in manuscript.

Place	Date	Hour	Summary of Events and Information	Remarks and references to Appendices
By Cmdr	1/4/17		1 section returning Brigade Camp	
POPE			1 section moving EVENDINGHE & 2 Section to bring mule to	
RINGHE	2/4/17		South East of	
			Huts	
	6/4/17		water to leper	
	7/4/17		to proceed to work but recalled a conveyed for hot dinner out from	
			3½ hrs word 4 miles from Cmd	
	8/4/17		Stop Training	
	11/4/17			
	12/4/17		5 Officer Training. Transport unended to HAZEBROUCK	
	13/4/17		" " " GOMME GONNEHEM	
	14/2/17			
	15/4/17		5 officer moved by train to BETHUNE	

Army Form C. 2118.

WAR DIARY
or
INTELLIGENCE SUMMARY.
(Erase heading not required.)

Instructions regarding War Diaries and Intelligence Summaries are contained in F.S. Regs., Part II. and the Staff Manual respectively. Title pages will be prepared in manuscript.

Place	Date	Hour	Summary of Events and Information	Remarks and references to Appendices
BETHUNE	16th		Officers visited the QUARRY SECTOR	
	17th		Company moved to NOYELLES	
NOYELLES	18th to 20th		Work on trenches went on much in accordance with programme it was found that it was quite impossible to do the work that could be left without communication trenches were impossible & all work that could be left without putting in was left for communication trenches	
	21st		"Bulls togger" with an action on clearing trenches	
	22nd 27th		Clearing trenches CHAPEL ALLEY Chapel Alley cleared as to be passable & worked in places to O.G.1. Working party 325 infantry 3 days 150 4 days	
			Stansfd STANSFIELD Rd cleared so as to be passable to O.G.1 km 150 Y.. 3 days 100 for 4 days	

WAR DIARY
or
INTELLIGENCE SUMMARY.

Army Form C. 2118.

(Erase heading not required.)

Place	Date	Hour	Summary of Events and Information	Remarks and references to Appendices
	24th		2 other O.R.s were employed & 3 other worked in town gun cushions were found
1 Heavy & 2 medium T M Emp were worked in
2. Drawing station finished
2 pumps repaired in NOYELLES & 1 installed in OB1
2. Horse troughs at SAILLY were repaired
40 Yds of tramway ballasted
The Reserve line wired from the FOSSEWAY to STAFFORD LANE entire
Entrances to the well dug out in O.B.4 timbered and entrance
started to dugout in DEVON LANE for machine gun detachment
marched to ROBECQ	WM Major RE OC 97 RE Coy

CONFIDENTIAL.

W A R   D I A R Y

of

97th Field Co. R.E. 21st Div.

———

March 1st to 31st. 1917.

———

VOL. XIX.

--

Army Form C. 2118.

91st Field Coy RE

WAR DIARY
or
INTELLIGENCE SUMMARY.
(Erase heading not required.)

Instructions regarding War Diaries and Intelligence Summaries are contained in F. S. Regs., Part II. and the Staff Manual respectively. Title pages will be prepared in manuscript.

Place	Date	Hour	Summary of Events and Information	Remarks and references to Appendices
ROBECQ	28/2/17		Left NOYELLES at 9.45 a.m. & arrived ROBECQ 3.0 p.m. Unit were supplied by open trucks	
ROBECQ	1/3/17		Rested	
"	2/3/17		Left ROBECQ at 10.0 a.m. & arrived GONNEHEM at 11.15 a.m.	
GONNEHEM	3/3/17		Rested. No 1 were preparing emplacement	
	5/3/17			
	6/3/17		joined by 1 Officer & NCOs & 96 Infantry 6 from each of forty battalions at BUSNES	
	7/3/17		Rested	
	8/3/17			
GONNEHEM	9/3/17		Left GONNEHEM 11.30 a.m. arrived FONTAINE LES HERMANS 5.0 p.m. Attached Infantry left BUSNES at 12.30 p.m. arrived FONTAINE LES HERMANS 4.45 p.m. They had the open trucks in 2 trips	
			MONNEVILLE arrived 1.45 p.m. the lorry made 2 trips	
FONTAINE	10/3/17		Left FONTAINE 10.50 a.m. arrived at HAUTECÔTE at 2.0 p.m. to billets	
MONNEVILLE	11/3/17		Left MONNEVILLE 7.40 a.m. arrived at HAUTECÔTE at 2.0 p.m. Lorry did 2 trips	
HAUTECÔTE	12/3/17		Left HAUTECÔTE 9.15 a.m. roads were soft with flour & rain at SIBIVILLE had to halt for 20 minutes as transport was stuck on the hill	

WAR DIARY
or
INTELLIGENCE SUMMARY
(Erase heading not required.)

Army Form C. 2118.

Place	Date	Hour	Summary of Events and Information	Remarks and references to Appendices
HALLOY	14/3/17		To avoid trouble on the hill all wagons were sent up with extra teams at ½ mile intervals this caused 1 hour delay.	
	22/3/17		At REBREUVIETTE a Front wireless said that the transport would strike on the third road at LUCHEUX or N by road via IVERGNY and caught up the Bde HQ transport at GROUCHES this transport had but 1 team on the other hill. Arrived at HALLOY 6.0 p.m.	
	23/3/17		"Lorry completed and left at 10.0 p.m. on 13/3/17	
	24/3/17		Hostel Started work on horses to every hat two in scout on pack saddles each box 3½ [?] laced with thistle to the 3 hind tires, armaments were also sold to the infantry detachment of proper exp.	
	25/3/17		Left HALLOY 9.45 a.m. arrived at BIENVILLERS au BOIS 2 p.m.	

WAR DIARY
or
INTELLIGENCE SUMMARY.

(Erase heading not required.)

Army Form C. 2118.

Instructions regarding War Diaries and Intelligence Summaries are contained in F. S. Regs., Part II. and the Staff Manual respectively. Title pages will be prepared in manuscript.

Place	Date	Hour	Summary of Events and Information	Remarks and references to Appendices
	26.3.17		Nos 1 2 & 4 Sections with the attached infantry marched to BOIRY ST MARTIN and bivouacked there, they spent a well earned rest. No 12 eleven at 11 p.m. No 3 completed the loose wpt to 15 long & 4 small, two battalion & 4 long & 2 small for the M G C.	
	27.3.17		No 1 continued with the well & also fitted up a flooded dug out for drawing water. No 2 should have begun job at BOISLEUX au MONT No 3 worked in wells in HUMBERCAMP also in huts for escape behind line. No 4 started continued work on a long bridge at BOISLEUX ST MARC The attached infantry mostly made a division arount a crater in BOIRY ST MARTIN	

Army Form C. 2118.

WAR DIARY
or
INTELLIGENCE SUMMARY.

(Erase heading not required.)

Instructions regarding War Diaries and Intelligence Summaries are contained in F.S. Regs., Part II. and the Staff Manual respectively. Title pages will be prepared in manuscript.

Place	Date	Hour	Summary of Events and Information	Remarks and references to Appendices
at	22/3/17 24/3/17		Continued work also No 2 started a new well at BOYELLES Continued work HUMBERCAMP finished and native tunnels started	
	30/3/17		No 3 French to BOIRY ST MARTIN 400 Yards strand the wood from BOISLEUX AUMONT to BOISLEUX ST MARE No 3 moved to BOIRY ST MARTIN went were continued & dugouts started to South of BOISLEUX St Mare Work continued but No 2 + 4 of day a supporting hand at T. 2 C also advanced Battalion H.Q.	
	31/3/17			

W iQu Major NR
O.S. 9 7th E NR

Vol 20 Confidential

WAR DIARY
of
97th Field Co. R.E.

VOL XX.

1 – 30 April 1917.

WAR DIARY or INTELLIGENCE SUMMARY

Army Form C. 2118.

97 - G RE

Place	Date	Hour	Summary of Events and Information	Remarks and references to Appendices
BOIRY ST MARTIN	1/4/17		No 1 worked on the long bridge at S.11 c.8.8. (Sheet 51B) with 100 attached Infantry. No 3 worked on a well at S.16 c.2.4 & on telegraph at S.16 a.1.7 No 2 & 4 Inft'y as support party & Battalion H.Q at T.21.d erected 5,100m. 2 Coys Infantry R.O.R worked on road from BIENVILLERS to MONCHY	
	2/4/17		No 1 ⎫ No 3 ⎬ continued work Attached Infantry 2 Coys P.O.R. No 2 assembled hour trans port for the D.A.C at the Sugar SUCRERIE. Completed & handed to own 3 pm. No 2 & two men went over with 137 M.F. in the attack with 15th Div. Made a strong point with 30 Inf. No 2 laid out main telephone & No 4 worked with the 11th N.F 4th division + No 2 went in No 4 with the 10th Yorks. No 1 completed the bridge & erected & filled holes in 300ᵈ of road at S.14.d.	
	3/4/17		The Infantry finished the approaches to the long bridge. No 2 made a division around the water at S.14.d.5.2 to the road leading S.W No 3 continued work	

WAR DIARY
or
INTELLIGENCE SUMMARY

Army Form C. 2118.

Place	Date	Hour	Summary of Events and Information	Remarks and references to Appendices
	4/4/17		No 1. Section starting to fill in the old road at S.19.c.9.8½. out to ways bolted and took the hand rail & spile of the long bridge and they had to go to repair this. No 2 completed the demolition of [illegible] work & house & latrines in the wire at S.19.b.9.1½ S.w.a.6.8½. S.14.c.2.7.2 No 3 continued work but couldn't enfaced stuff. to 1 day out of the wall No 4 commenced w long bridge at S.12 b.9.7 20 ft filling w' bridge The Infantry worked on the road to BOISLEUX au MONT	
	5/4/17		No 1 refaired the bridge & filled & drained the afternoon when they had work No 2 started clearing & draining the road from S.14.a.7.2. to BOISLEUX au MONT No 3 finished the wall & continued work	

WAR DIARY or INTELLIGENCE SUMMARY

Army Form C. 2118.

Place	Date	Hour	Summary of Events and Information	Remarks and references to Appendices
			No 4 continued work	
			The attached Infantry worked on the filling in and the driving in of S.10.c.9.3½ & continued on the work read	
			2 Coys of 2/2 London n worked on the road from BIENVILLERS to MONCHY	
	6/4/17		No 1 continued work	
			No 2 replied the trench S.9.c.6.3. which had caved in	
			No 3 continued work on dugouts & passing to join to No 2	
			No 4 continued work	
			The attached Infantry employed the enemy	
			2 Coys 2/2 London continued work	
	7/4/17		No 1 made a decauville round the trench at S.6.d.7.2.	
			No 2 & Infantry employed the cleaning & clearing of the road to BOISLEUX au MONT	

WAR DIARY
or
INTELLIGENCE SUMMARY

Army Form C. 2118.

(Erase heading not required.)

Place	Date	Hour	Summary of Events and Information	Remarks and references to Appendices
	8/4/17		No 4 completed the bridge. The transport and sundry parties arrived from BIENVILLERS & the 12th B. had over the work. No 2 continued with dug outs. No 1 made 21 cuts for entering wire for 6 & 13 Bn. No 3 continued with dug outs. 2 wagons & 4 men went to BIENVILLERS & BERLES to return tools.	
	9/4/17		½ the attached Infantry worked on the roads in the village age & ½ returned tools. The sections filled out the battalion wagons with tools his errand during the 13th N.F. completed 12th N.F failed to carry 80thm 1st Lines complete. 10th Yorks supplied with picks tools & out filled out.	

WAR DIARY
or
INTELLIGENCE SUMMARY.

Army Form C. 2118.

(Erase heading not required.)

Instructions regarding War Diaries and Intelligence Summaries are contained in F.S. Regs., Part II. and the Staff Manual respectively. Title pages will be prepared in manuscript.

Place	Date	Hour	Summary of Events and Information	Remarks and references to Appendices
	10/4/17		worked on road to BOISLEUX ST MARE & also filled & levelled troughs with AI Sg AIS-C & supplied troops with cattle drinking troughs for 6 AIB.	
	11/4/17		25 Inf & 4 section worked on emption on ARRAS-BAPAUME Rd through BOYELLES. 1 section & 75 infantry on the road to BOIRY BECQUERELLE.	
	12/4/17		No1 improved the approaches to the bridge at Tu 9.8. No 2 sect. continued work on ARRAS-BAPAUME Rd. Tu Infantry worked on the road through BOISLEUX au MONT.	
	13/4/17		No1 & 75 Inf. worked on the road to BOIRY BECQUERELLE & made a road for tracking lorries to BOISLEUX au MONT station. No 2. 3. 4. & 25 Inf worked on the ARRAS BAPAUME Rd.	
	14/4/17		No 1, No 4, the attached infantry & 1 Eng Pioneer worked on the road to BOIRY BECQUERELLE. No 2 & No 3 worked on the ARRAS BAPAUME Rd & BOISLEUX ST MARC - BOYELLES Rd. In the evening the whole turned out to mend up roads in the villages which had been very much broken by heavy	

#353 Wt. W3544/1454 700,000 5/15 D. D. & L. A.D.S.S./Forms/C. 2118.

WAR DIARY
INTELLIGENCE SUMMARY
(Erase heading not required.)

Army Form C. 2118.

Place	Date	Hour	Summary of Events and Information	Remarks and references to Appendices
	15/4/17		No 1 worked on the withdrawal to BOISLEUX au MONT station No. 2, 3, 4 & the Infantry on the BOIRY BECQUERELLE road. No. 2 worked on the ARRAS–BAPAUME Rd & the BOISLEUX au MONT ST MARC–BOYELLES Rd	
	16/4/17 17/4/17		Both to a NISSEN HUT at HAMELINCOURT	
	18/4/17 19/4/17		Solving stones	
	25/4/17		Road from BOISLEUX au MONT to BOISLEUX ST MARC, and having an old well at BOISLEUX au MONT with bricks, also picking smaller stones lower down the hill, this was handed over 11 chef to 132 AT Coy R.E.	
	26/4/17		Marched to BOIRY BECQUERELLE left 9.45 a.m. arrived 11.0 a.m. billeted in dug outs in sunken road	

Army Form C. 2118.

WAR DIARY
or
INTELLIGENCE SUMMARY.
(Erase heading not required.)

Instructions regarding War Diaries and Intelligence Summaries are contained in F. S. Regs. Part II. and the Staff Manual respectively. Title pages will be prepared in manuscript.

Place	Date	Hour	Summary of Events and Information	Remarks and references to Appendices
RORY BECQUEREL	27/4/17		Work on defences see details attached	
	30/4/17		Sergt HAWARD R.E. was wounded by a fracture at No 7 work on 28/4/17 — at No 9 — on 30/4/17 Sapr Holdcroun wounded	Wilson Major RE O.C. 171st E.R.R 1/5/17

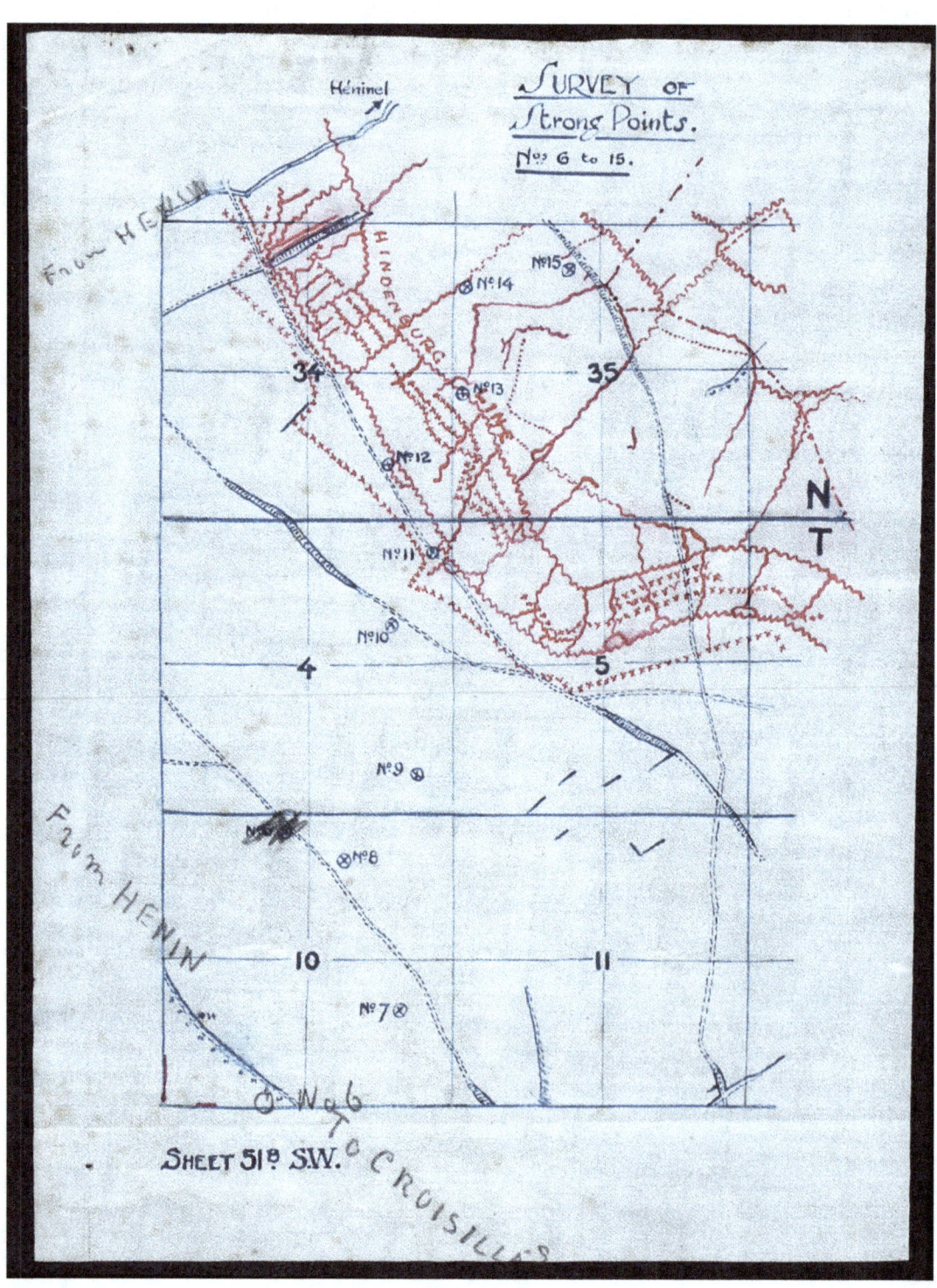

Work to be done by 97th Co. R.E. &
   D. Coy. Pioneers.

Work to consist of a line of Strongpoints each point to be able to hold 40 men and to give each man 2 firing positions, to contain bomb stores latrines and shell slits.

The Trench to be wide enough for men to pass and to have a fire step.

Wire to be inconspicuous and to surround the work with an entrance gap at the back not to be heavily wired but to be at least 8' wide.

Foreground to be cleared giving a good field of fire and leaving no dead ground between works except Nos 11 and 12, and 11 and 13. This dead piece is to be covered by an ∧ piece of wire

Nos 6 to 11 to be joined up with a wire fence this fence to have gaps about every 250x for carts covered on the enemy's side by a single fence the position of the gap to be shewn by   o — o — o — o   boards.

—o——o——o——o   o——o——o——o—
            ↕12'
            ←-12'-→
—o——o——o——o   o——o——o——o—

     White board   White Board

At about 80x a gap for Infantry

   —o——o——o   o——o——o—

    —o——o   o   o   o

The work will be allotted as follows:—
Nº 6 (T.10. a. 9.9.) + wire to Nº 7.   Nº 4 Section
Nº 7 (T.10. d. 7.7.) ⎫
Nº 8 (T.10. b. 3.7.) ⎭ + wire to Nº 9. D. Coy. 14th Northd Fusiliers
                                              (Pioneers).
Nº 9 (T.4. d. 8.3.) + wire to Nº 10 - Nº 3 Section + 25 Infantry.
Nº 10 (T.4. b. 6.3.) + wire to HINDENBURG LINE
Nº 11 (T.4. b. 9.8.) ⎫
Nº 12 (N.34. d. 6.4.) ⎬ + wiring to cover dead ground by D. Coy.
Nº 13 (N.35. c. 1.9.) ⎭   14th N.F. (Pioneers)
Nº 14 (N.35. a. 1.6.)   40 Infantry
Nº 15 (N.35. a. 8.7.)   Nº 1 Section + 25 Infantry.

                                       W. Wisher
                                       Major R.E.

Vol 21

CONFIDENTIAL.

WAR DIARY
OF
97th Field Co. R.E.

MAY 1917.

Army Form C. 2118.

WAR DIARY
or
INTELLIGENCE SUMMARY.

(Erase heading not required.)

11th Field Ambulance R8

Instructions regarding War Diaries and Intelligence Summaries are contained in F. S. Regs., Part II. and the Staff Manual respectively. Title pages will be prepared in manuscript.

Place	Date	Hour	Summary of Events and Information	Remarks and references to Appendices
BOIRY BECQUERELLE	1/5/17		Work on strong points continued	
	2/5/17		Ditto	
	3/5/17		Paraded at 5.0 a.m and proceeded to the trench which had been used as a jumping off trench for the assault on HINDENBURG LINE & worked there to consolidated it. The end objective but in this was not been returned to even at 9.0 p.m. Section had at 9.30 p.m (1 man wounded	
	4/5/17		Work from the BROWN LINE from the HINDENBURG SUPPORT TRENCH to the embankment 100 & double form 6 kingposts & 2 dugouts (Night work) (1 man killed)	
	5/5/17		Work from No 11 S.P. to No 15.	
	6/5/17		GREYST was fire stepped & work continued finishing the head pin	
			GREYST to No 15 work the latter was nearly work	
	7/9/17		GREYST was wired & the head joining it to 15 work completed (night work)	
	8/5/17		work from 13 to 15 work a run of communication hurt & along hurt to GREYST from 15 work (this work except from 15 work to GREYSE	

Army Form C. 2118.

WAR DIARY
or
INTELLIGENCE SUMMARY.

(Erase heading not required.)

Instructions regarding War Diaries and Intelligence Summaries are contained in F. S. Regs., Part II. and the Staff Manual respectively. Title pages will be prepared in manuscript.

Place	Date	Hour	Summary of Events and Information	Remarks and references to Appendices
BOIRY	9/5/17		Night work dug out S & S hund for S.P. C.6, C.7, C.8, C.9, C.10	
BECOURELLE	10/5/17		Worked nothing in trench to S.P.S, S.P. known & R.V.9 comp. Track dulled & marginal arrival on each side. Night work wiring the S.P.O & added to them to increase their field of fire in enstern direction	
	11/5/17		Finished the S.P.s and tried to join new trenches to a jumping off near PVE LANE til front. The specialles damaged	
	12/5/17		Marched to RANSART at 3.0 pm	
RANSART	13/5/17		Rested	
	14/5/17		2 Sections at work huthing 10th Yorks at HENDECOURT	
	15/5/17		ditto ditto	
	16/5/17		1 Section ditto. 2 Sections collecting material for 11th & 13th N.F. camp. 12th & 13th Pioneers to do R. work 1 Section musketry	
	17/5/17		Monthly order friends School 7 man went to work on Corps rifle range	
	18/5/17		2 Sections made a practice trench for the troops to practice assaulting 1 Section collecting stones for 1st Line dump	

Army Form C. 2118.

WAR DIARY
or
INTELLIGENCE SUMMARY.
(Erase heading not required.)

Instructions regarding War Diaries and Intelligence Summaries are contained in F. S. Regs., Part II. and the Staff Manual respectively. Title pages will be prepared in manuscript.

Place	Date	Hour	Summary of Events and Information	Remarks and references to Appendices
RANSART	19/5/17		No 1 Section collected stores for 10th Yorks Reconnaissance for preparing for work	
	20/5/17		Slush	
	21/5/17		Inspection by N.C.R. No 1 afterwards went forward went on work for an Artillery Emp't at HENDECOURT	
	22/5/17		# 1 section on Artillery Emp't (1 in 1st line Emp't & on 10th Yorks outpost) Laying out Inspection by G.O.C. 21st Division 1 section working a human shield & went on fatigue to right wing & billets in RANSART	
	23/5/17		2 Sections working on human shield & went on work at BLAIREVILLE Infantry outposts field gun pits dugouts etc	
	24/5/17		ditto but infantry detached from sections for training in infantry duties by their battalion previously Men as required by C.C's	
	25/5/17		ditto	
	26/5/17		100 t'ls powder charges exploded up in 3" and fired with time fuze to respirated troops in 12th N.F. practice attack	

Army Form C. 2118.

WAR DIARY
or
INTELLIGENCE SUMMARY.
(Erase heading not required.)

Instructions regarding War Diaries and Intelligence Summaries are contained in F. S. Regs., Part II. and the Staff Manual respectively. Title pages will be prepared in manuscript.

Place	Date	Hour	Summary of Events and Information	Remarks and references to Appendices
RANSART	27/5/17		Sunday a holiday	
	28/5/17		1 section marching & section on BLAIREVILLE CAMP	
	29/5/17		1 section & drivers marching & wnt for TOWM MAJOR RANSART. 3 Sections for work at BLAIREVILLE. Infants for talks and the morning section & drivers reflecting employed & making emplmts for 300 mm at BLAIREVILLE enemy land room 6"	
	30/5/17		Remain in billets	
	31/5/17		Marched to ST LEGER and from camped at JUDAS FARM leaving 9 O.S. um & carrying 30 km bridging stores were attended at HAMELINCOURT	

31/5/17
Maire Major NR
OE-97 PR & NR

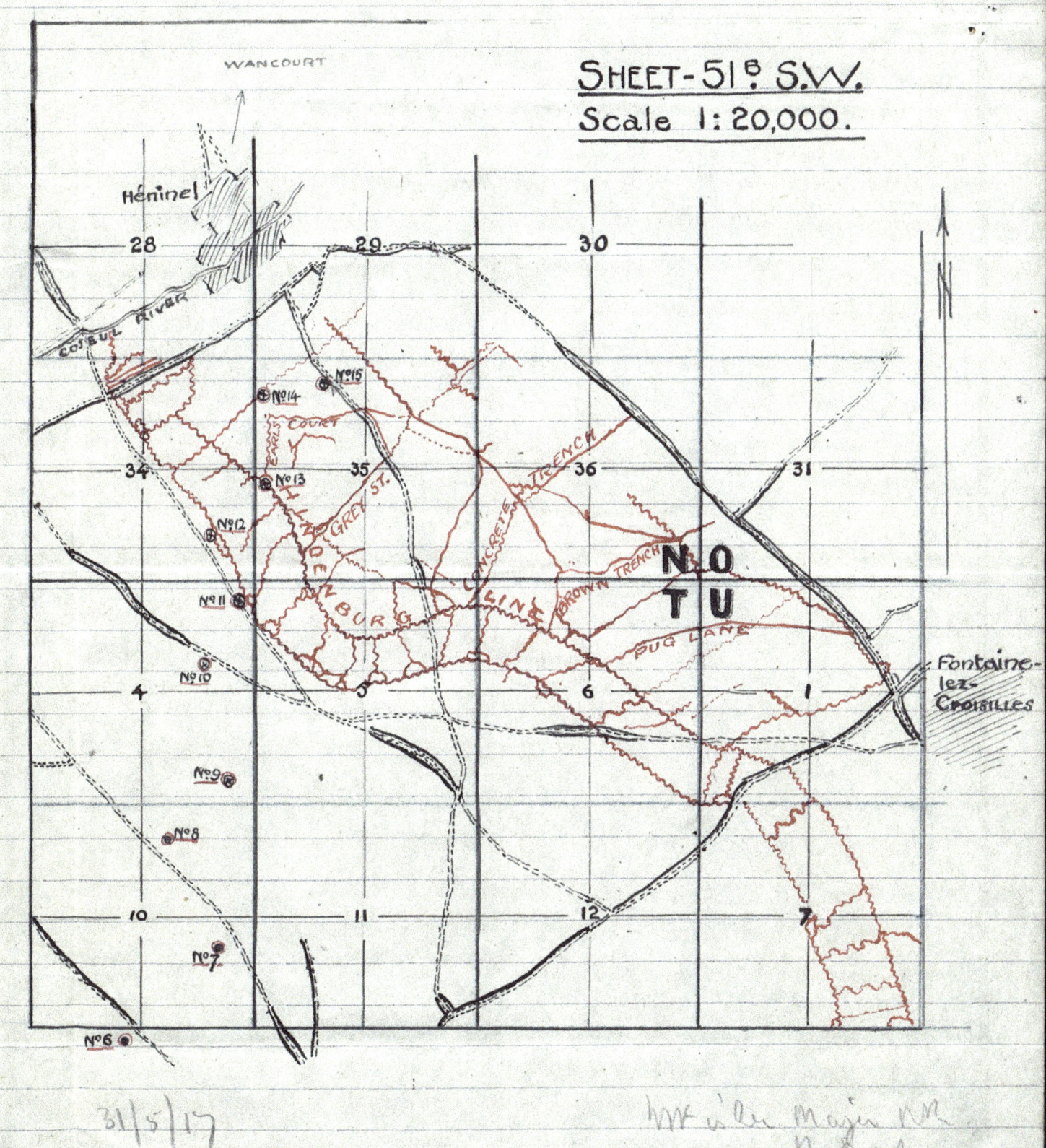

Confidential

War Diary
of
91st Field Co. R.E.

June 1 - 30. 1917.

WAR DIARY
or
INTELLIGENCE SUMMARY.

Army Form C. 2118.

9th Field Coy R.E.

Place	Date	Hour	Summary of Events and Information	Remarks and references to Appendices
JOOKS FARM	31/5/15 1/6/15		Stores sent up at night to RUSSELLS GARDEN. Work on dugouts commenced at 6.0 a.m. on number of dugouts in 4 strips of sections 15 long with roofs of a leading & running front. Chambers 6'6" x 6' x 4' by an 20' for dug. (1 Sapper man wounded with gun shot).	
	3/6/15		12 more. All empty end entrances strutted & boarding cut in and a placed	
	5/6/15		Mine craters collected & engaged up to BUNG TRENCH & Turtle arranged & opened up ready for emerging work. Cont shelled from 9.15 a.m. to 10.0 p.m 2 teams men 22 hours slightly wounded & 1 wagon & various stores damaged.	
	6/6/15		An Officer proceeded to supervise the deepening of LUMP LANE & on to survey for forward saps work on dugouts continued	
	7/6/15		Supervision of deepening of LUMP LANE continued also the dugouts continued 1 Col Infantry accidentally wounded when carrying stores. This was done by a bayonet sticking out from the trench side.	

Army Form C. 2118.

WAR DIARY
or
INTELLIGENCE SUMMARY.
(Erase heading not required.)

Instructions regarding War Diaries and Intelligence Summaries are contained in F. S. Regs., Part II. and the Staff Manual respectively. Title pages will be prepared in manuscript.

Place	Date	Hour	Summary of Events and Information	Remarks and references to Appendices
ST JUDAS FARM	9/6/17		Work on dug-out in which 3 N.E.'s wounded marching up & Infantry carrying stores one since died of wounds.	
	10/6/17		Work continued camp moved down the hill to the valley out of sight	
	11/6/17		ditto	
	12/6/17		ditto	
	13/6/17		Work stopped for talks from 12 M N 12/13 till 6.0 a.m 14th	
	14/6/17		Work continued 2 thunder for E.O.s & a new entrance started but work could not be started until 6.0 p.m a new entrance being	
			to the tortile pm	
	15/6/17		Dug-out dummy cut entrances broomed and left at 1·30 a.m 16/6/17 New entrance incomplete party should have left at # midnight but were prevented by hostile fire	
	16/6/17		4 tons standing by to consolidate	
	17/6/17		Work restarted at 7.0 p.m	

WAR DIARY or INTELLIGENCE SUMMARY

Army Form C. 2118.

Place	Date	Hour	Summary of Events and Information	Remarks and references to Appendices
Nr ST LEGER	18/6/17		Work continued, but very much interrupted, the party had to attend to one of the Infantry attack to 3 times the wagons with stores were not set up owing to the bush + damp being pulled down. carts went	
			2/LT. HOWORTH. G.E. R.E. joined from 132 A.T. Coy R.E.	
	19/6/17		Work continued 7.30 p.m	
	20/6/17		Marched to NELLACOURT leaving 8.30 a.m + arriving 11.15 a.m	
	21/6/17		Cleaning up + digging sample pits for the Infantry course	
	22		Work on camps. Drill. Digging sample trenches for Infantry course. Instruction in military engineering. Major J.T. FISHER proceeded to England on leave	
	23		Work on brigade camps. Drill. Finished sample trenches	
	24		Sunday — church parade.	
	25		Drill. First day of Infantry course of instruction. Salving material from old works	
	26		Drill. First day of Infantry course. Salvage.	

Army Form C. 2118.

WAR DIARY
or
INTELLIGENCE SUMMARY.
(Erase heading not required.)

Place	Date	Hour	Summary of Events and Information	Remarks and references to Appendices
BELLACOURT	June 27		Company drill, salvage.	
"	28		Company drill, salvage.	
"	29		Baths	
"	30		No Company (dismounted men 9a.m. infantry) moved to Boiry Becquerelle by 60cm Railway leaving Exeter Siding 8.45 a.m. arriving 10 a.m. Transport travelled by road arriving at 10.30 a.m.	
BOIRY BECQUERELLE	1			

Plumbley
Lieut RE.
for O.C. 97th Field Coy R.E.

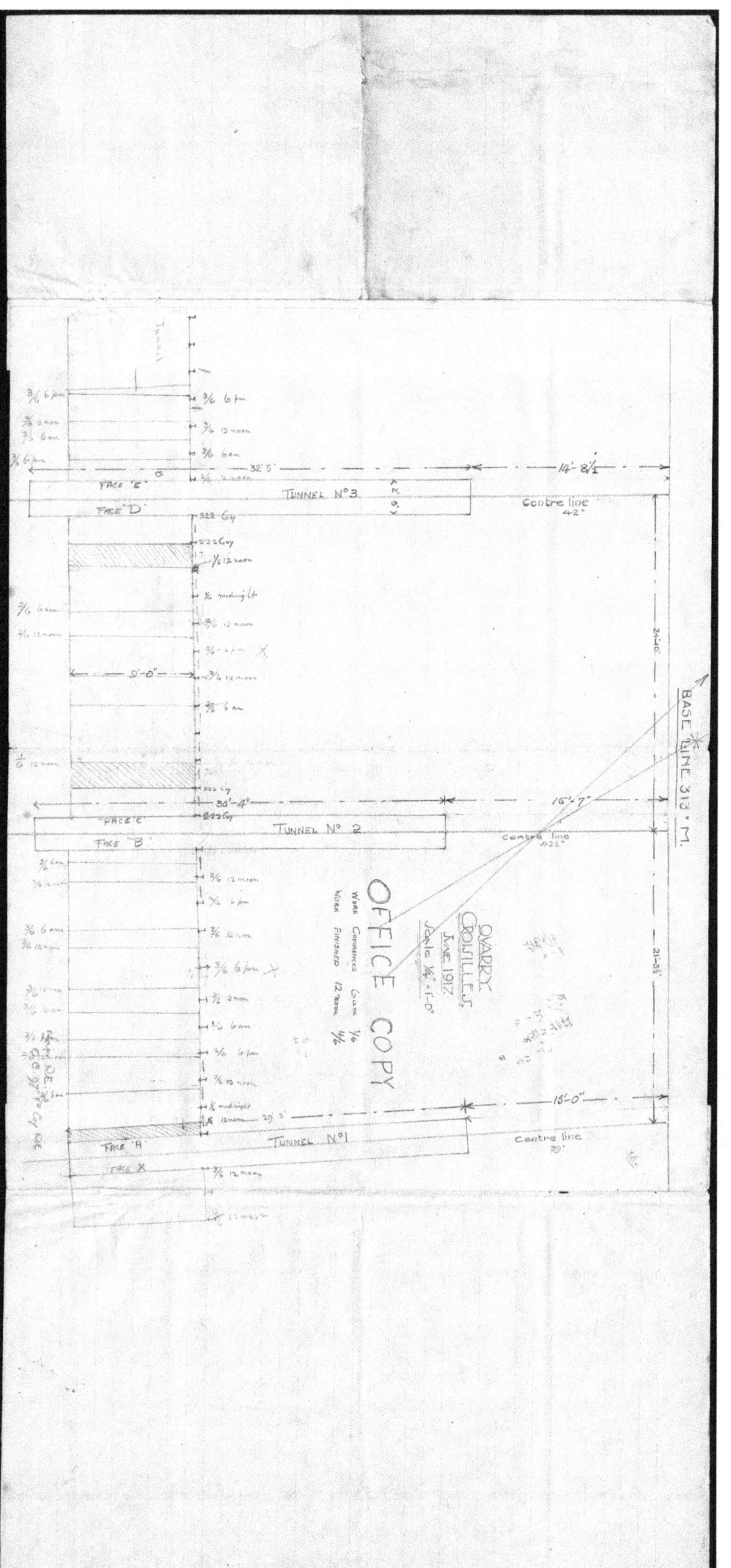

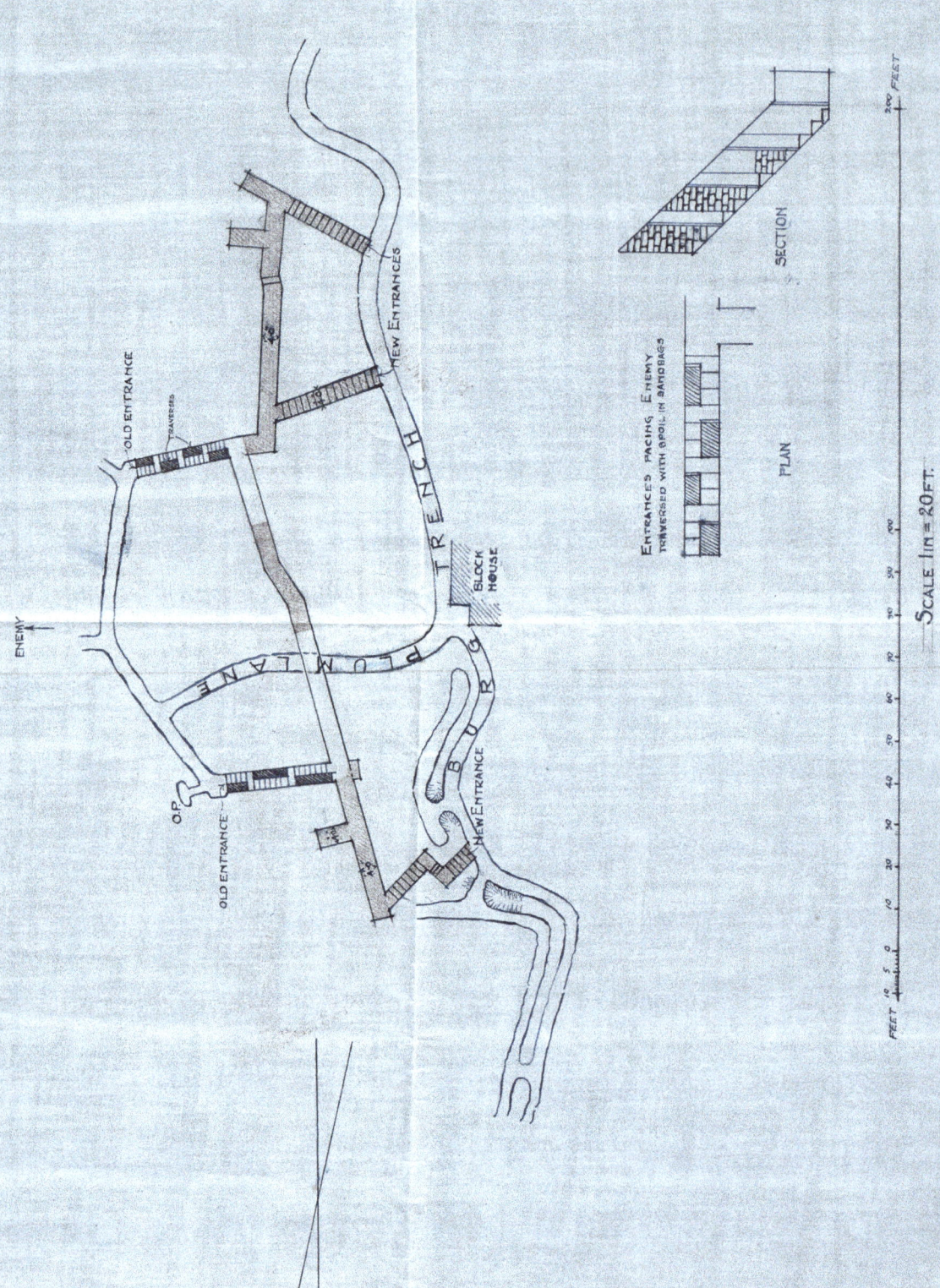

Vol 23

Confidential

War Diary
of.
91st Field Co R.E.

1st – 31st July 1917

Army Form C. 2118.

WAR DIARY
or
INTELLIGENCE SUMMARY. 97th Field Coy R.E.

(Erase heading not required.)

Instructions regarding War Diaries and Intelligence Summaries are contained in F. S. Regs., Part II. and the Staff Manual respectively. Title pages will be prepared in manuscript.

Place	Date	Hour	Summary of Events and Information	Remarks and references to Appendices
BOIRY-BECQUERELLE	July 1		Work commenced on trenches. No 1 section clearing tunnel in SHAFT TRENCH. No 2 supporting HIND TRENCH. No 3 in camp and reserve battalion drills. No 4 on RESERVE LINE. Lt G.E. HOWORTH. M.C. R.E. proceeded to join 214TH (A.T.) Coy R.E.	
	2		Work continued	
	3		Work continued	
	4		Work continued MAJOR. J.T. FISHER returned from leave	
	5		Work continued	
	6		Work commenced as on attached programme. i) H. CARNELLEY. R.E. proceeded on leave to England. 1 Section 97th Coy R.E. to attached Infantry cerem to live in	A
			SHAFT TRENCH	
	10		Leg bath	
	11		Leg bath	
	13		Leg bath	
	17A		Pte Marsh 13th NF wounded	
	16		Work commenced on new programme	
	19 N		Leg bath	
	15 N		Leg bath	
	20 N		Wld Cy bath	
	24 R			
	26 A		Pte Marsh 13 NF returned to duty	
	28 A		Marched to HAMELINCOURT arrived 12 noon	

WAR DIARY
or
INTELLIGENCE SUMMARY

Army Form C. 2118.

Place	Date	Hour	Summary of Events and Information	Remarks and references to Appendices
	28th to 30th		15 wmf at STALEY Ridge. ITM Enlargement of off SWALLOW AVENUE with a curved trunk. 10 Passage through the HINDENBURG ww. 6.1 man Shelter at entry funk	
	29th 30th		No 1 Section completed the & engine room aft the tunnel to 26'6". No 3 made 116 ventures and improved horse standings & worked on return at 3 water points. No 1 & No 4 worked in the workshop & etc on a new R.E. Yard.	
	31st		B.M's for 1.3.84. H.Q. & Infantry	

Walter Major RE
OC 97th EWn

WAR DIARY
or
INTELLIGENCE SUMMARY.

Army Form C. 2118.

(Erase heading not required.)

Place	Date	Hour	Summary of Events and Information	Remarks and references to Appendices

Summary of Work done

BUSH Trench duckboarded & revetted for 410'

PUG AVENUE ———— 981'ˣ revetted 470'ᵈ

DODO dugout 40' of chamber + 28' of stairs

MG Dugout 62' ———— 52' of stairs

M.C. Gun pit 12' of tunnel

2 chungo fired in an abandoned post

1 Hut in PUG AVENUE

1 Felling gate in SNIPE TR

1 Lewis gun well & several approaches in NIVEN Road

Bde HQ Men + Cookhouse cut out in bank of sunken road

64 Gas & Hunish panel

29 Shift huts in tunnel

4 chambers off the tunnel   (2 9'×9'×6', 1 4'×8'×6', 1 9'×14'×6')

Programme of Work.   (commencing 7-7-17).

Right Battalion   Wire BUCK TRENCH.   ½ Coy 8 days
        400 Yds Wire   (½ ton)
        250 Pickets   (1 ton)

    Dig out and revet BUCK TRENCH.
        1 Coy. 10 days
        150 Duck Boards   (3½ tons)
        500 Sheets Iron   (7 tons)
        1000 ʇ Iron Pickets   (5 tons)

    Dig out CLAW TRENCH. 400ˣ 8 days
        120 Duck boards   (3 tons)
        400 Sheets Iron   (6 tons)
        800 Pickets   (4 tons)

  No 1 Section   Trimming up Entrances
        20 Cases (2 tons)

Support Batt.
    Wire BUSH TRENCH.   ½ Coy 8 days
        400 Yards Wire   (½ ton)
        250 Pickets   (1 ton)

    Duckboard & Revet SWALLOW LANE   1 Coy. 16 days
        240 Duckboards   (6 tons)
        800 Sheets Iron   (12 tons)
        1600 ʇ Iron Pickets   (8 tons)

  No 2 Section   BUSH TRENCH.   7 days.
        150 duckboards   (3½ tons)
        500 Sheets Iron   (7 tons)
        1000 ʇ Iron Pickets   (5 tons)

Reserve Batt.   CONCRETE TRENCH.   1 Coy 16 days
        240 Duckboards   (6 tons)
        800 Sheets Iron   (12 ,,)
        1600 Pickets   (8 ,,)

    FULDNER LANE   4 days
        60 Duckboards   (1½ tons)
        200 Sheets Iron   (3 tons)
        400 Pickets   (2 tons)

P.T.O.

<u>Pioneers</u>	THRUSH TRENCH.	1 Platoon
	60 duckboards	(1½ tons)
	200 Sheets Iron	(3 tons)
	400 Pickets	(2 tons)
<u>Hd Qrs. Left Batt.</u>	AVENUE TRENCH	12 days
	70 duck boards	(½ tons)
	500 sheets iron	(7 ")
	1000 T Iron Pickets	(5 ")
No 3 Section	clearing dugout entrances SHAFT TRENCH northwards	
	20 Cases (2 tons) daily	
No 4. Section	New shaft in DODO TRENCH. } 8 cases 1 ton	
	" " SWALLOW LANE } daily	
T.Ms.	New dug-out & emplacement 3 weeks	
	4 Cases ½ ton daily.	

Programme of Work. 16-7-17.

Trench	Unit	Strength	Nature of Work	Start	Finish	Trench Boards	X P M Sheets	Litora	6x4 Dugout Frames	Weight Tons	Weight per day Tons	Remarks
CONCRETE RESERVE	Support Batn 1 Company	70	Revet and Trench-board 400 yds	20.7.17	28.7.17	150	400	800		10	1⅛	
BROWN SUPPORT	Reserve Batn 2 CoyS	180	Do 1000 yds	20.7.17	1.8.17	350	1000	2000		25	2¼	
HORN TRENCH	Support Btn ½ Coy	35	Revet 500 yds	20.7.17	31.7.17		500	1000		8	¾	
LAW TR. from PUG AV. Posts	98th Coy Detachmt	70	Revet & Trench-board 200 yds	20.7.17	23.7.17	70	200	400		5	1¼	
PUSH TR.	No.2 Section		Do 300 yds	24.7.17	29.7.17	100	300	600		7½	¾	No.2 Section Stopped this Work on 28.7.17 to commence Engine Room Chamber.
FIRST AVE. from Batt HQ southwards	Support Batn 1 Coy	70	Do 400 yds	20.7.17	28.7.17	150	400	800		10	1⅛	
from Coy HQ to CURTAIN TR.	½ Coy 14th N.F.	100	Do 300 yds	21.7.17	26.7.17	100	300	600		7½	1¼	
SWIFT TR. to PIPE TR.	½ Coy 14th N.F.	50	Do 200 yds	25.7.17	29.7.17	70	200	400		5	1	
CONCRETE DUGOUT	½ Coy 14th N.F.	50	Tunnel 40 feet	20.7.17	24.7.17				50	5	1	
NEW DUGOUT & M.G.	No 1 & 3 Sections	60	Tunnel 80 feet & 25 feet for Gun emplacement	20.7.17	27.7.17				115	11½	1½	
ODD DUGOUT	No.4 Section	30	Tunnel 35 feet	20.7.17	27.7.17				42	4¼	½	
WOOD TR. DUGOUT	½ Coy 14th N.F.	70	Tunnel (?) say 40 ft	25.7.17	5.8.17				(?170)	(?17)	1	
LAW SUPPORT	½ Coy 14th N.F.	50	Revet and Trenchboard 200 yds	20.7.17	24.7.17	70	200	400		5	1	
SWALLOW to SWIFT	98th Coy Detachmt	70	Revet and Trenchboard 500 yds	24.7.17	1.8.17	170	500	1000		12½	1¼	
			Remainder on Wiring and improving posts — about 1000 sandbags daily, 10 sheets of small shelters, 100 coils of wire, 400 screw pickets								3¼	

Original

Confidential

War Diary
of
97th Field Co. R.E.

August 1st - 31st 1917.

Army Form C. 2118.

WAR DIARY
or
INTELLIGENCE SUMMARY.
(Erase heading not required.)

Instructions regarding War Diaries and Intelligence Summaries are contained in F. S. Regs., Part II. and the Staff Manual respectively. Title pages will be prepared in manuscript.

Place	Date	Hour	Summary of Events and Information	Remarks and references to Appendices
HAMELINCOURT	1/8/17		Work continued in Camp Workshops and on new R.E. Yard at BOYELLES. No 1 Section relieved No 3 Section in SHAFT TRENCH.	
"	2.8.17		Digging of Company Horse Commenced at MONDICOURT. Making Concertinas as continued. also new R.E. Yard. Work Commenced on Wells at No 4 Water Point MOYENVILLE and at MAISON ROUGE.	
"	3.8.17		Work continued on Wells, also on Horse Lines and the making of Concertinas. Work continued.	
"	4.8.17		"	
"	5.8.17		"	
"	6.8.17		Baths for 1. 2. 3 & 4 H.Q. Sections and attached Infantry. Work continued on Wells, &c..	
"	7.8.17		"	
"	8.8.17		"	
"	9.8.17		No 1 Section relieved No 4 Section in ST LEGER.	
"	10.8.17		No 4 Section took over all work in the workshops and No 3 Section the new R.E. Yard.	
"	11.8.17		Work continued.	

Army Form C. 2118.

WAR DIARY
or
INTELLIGENCE SUMMARY.

(Erase heading not required.)

Instructions regarding War Diaries and Intelligence Summaries are contained in F. S. Regs., Part II. and the Staff Manual respectively. Title pages will be prepared in manuscript.

Place	Date	Hour	Summary of Events and Information	Remarks and references to Appendices
HAPLINCOURT	12.8.17		Baths for Nos 2, 3, 4 H.Q. Drs. Sections & attached Infantry. 2nd Lieut. P.P. Sage home to UK.	
"	13.8.17		Work commenced at ERVILLERS on Nissen huts for 1st Lincolns Regt. H.Q. at B.13.c.2.1 (57C NW) and 10th Yorkshire Regt. Camps at B.13.b.3.3 (57C NW). Also on horse standings for 110th Bde & 64th Bde at B.19.b.6.5. Other work continued.	
"	14.8.17		Work continued.	
"	15.8.17		Do.	
"	16.8.17		Do.	
"	17.8.17		Do.	
"	18.8.17		Do.	
"	19.8.17		Baths for Nos 2, 3, 4, H.Q. Brs. Sections & attached Infantry. No 2 Section relieved No 1 Section at ST. LEGER.	
"	20.8.17		Work continued. No 1 Section relieved No 3 Section at MOYENNEVILLE and finished same, afterwards working on huts for 7th Leicesters.	
"	21.8.17		Work continued.	
"	22.8.17		Do.	
"	23.8.17		Do. 2nd Lieut. P.P. Sage returned from leave.	
"	24.8.17		Do.	
"	25.8.17		Do. Capt. V. Lowe left for Training Camp Rouen.	

Army Form C. 2118.

WAR DIARY
or
INTELLIGENCE SUMMARY.
(Erase heading not required.)

Instructions regarding War Diaries and Intelligence Summaries are contained in F. S. Regs., Part II. and the Staff Manual respectively. Title pages will be prepared in manuscript.

Place	Date	Hour	Summary of Events and Information	Remarks and references to Appendices
HAMELINCOURT	26.8.17		Baths for Company at MOYENNEVILLE	
"	27.8.17		Company marched to DAINVILLE L.29.c.2.0.(57°). Leaving at 10.0 am and arriving at 3.0 p.m.; attached Infantry rejoined their respective battalions. Lieut. G.C. Rowe on leave to U.K.	
AINVILLE	28.8.17		Company at Section Drill: remainder of day spent on roofing and improving billets and horse-lines.	
"	29.8.17		Work on billets continued. Coy at Section Drill. All Gas helmets & respirators inspected. Nos 1 & 2 Sections harness inspected.	
"	30.8.17		Work on billets continued. Drill and Kit Inspection. Nos 3 & 4 Section Harness inspected.	
"	31.8.17		Nos 1 & 2 Section Pontooning Drill; Nos 3 & 4 Sections Route March and Selection of sites for strong-points. Head Quarters Section Harness inspected.	

W.Wild
Major R.E.
O.C. 97th Field Coy R.E.

CONFIDENTIAL

WAR DIARY
of.
97th Field Co RE

Septr. 1917

Vol 25

Army Form C. 2118.

WAR DIARY
or
INTELLIGENCE SUMMARY.
(Erase heading not required.)

Instructions regarding War Diaries and Intelligence Summaries are contained in F. S. Regs., Part II. and the Staff Manual respectively. Title pages will be prepared in manuscript.

Place	Date	Hour	Summary of Events and Information	Remarks and references to Appendices
DAINVILLE	1/9/17		Drill etc	
	2/9/17		Baths	
	3/9/17		Drill etc	
	4/9/17			
	5/9/17		Made 18 large latrines for 3 platoons & 4 small for 1 platoon	
			20 stitch for YUKON Push & shields of ordnance grass	
	6/9/17		Transport left 2.30 p.m. cyclists 4.0 p.m. & Support 6.0 p.m. in Lorries & arrived at AUBIGNY. Cyclists & other at 9.30 p.m.	
	7/9/17		Detrained HOPOUTRE 6.30 a.m. marched off 7.30 and Support & cyclists in Lorries. Transport breakfasted at BUSSEBOOM at 7.0 a.m. marched off again at 9.0 a.m. arrived at 11.0 a.m. at RIDGE WOOD	
RIDGEWOOD	8/9/17		Erecting NISSEN HUTS	

Army Form C. 2118.

WAR DIARY
or
INTELLIGENCE SUMMARY.
(Erase heading not required.)

Instructions regarding War Diaries and Intelligence Summaries are contained in F. S. Regs., Part II. and the Staff Manual respectively. Title pages will be prepared in manuscript.

Place	Date	Hour	Summary of Events and Information	Remarks and references to Appendices
RIDGE WOOD	9/9/16		Enemy hut	
	10/9/16		1 Section on MIDDLESEX road with P.O. Prisoners	
	11/9/16	2½	ditto	
	12/9/16	2½	ditto	
	13/9/16	2	ditto 2 off of Pioneers + the sappers did 570' of double hurt plant	Pertaining Relent Walter of 1 DICKEBUSH storage started
	14/9/16		used during this period	
	15/9/17		Work on hut RIDGE WOOD camp completed total extd 21 Nissen huts	completed 12 & 1 double hut
	16/9/17		also total stores of clothes shelters assembled at DICKEBUSH Stores	
	17/9/17		thirty	
	18/9/17		Work commenced on SCOTTISH WOOD camp 2 sections returned for work at 11.0 a.m. funerals for work at 11.0 p.m. + 4.0 p.m. but went cancelled afterwards	

Army Form C. 2118.

WAR DIARY
or
INTELLIGENCE SUMMARY.

(Erase heading not required.)

Instructions regarding War Diaries and Intelligence Summaries are contained in F. S. Regs., Part II. and the Staff Manual respectively. Title pages will be prepared in manuscript.

Place	Date	Hour	Summary of Events and Information	Remarks and references to Appendices
RIDGE WOOD	23/9/17		1 section hutting in SCOTTISH WOOD	
	24/9/17		2 sections laying tramline in SANCTUARY WOOD (1 sapper wounded)	
			1 section pushing up tramline from VALLEY COTTAGES	
			2 sections hutting	
			1 section completing tramline as far as SANCTUARY WOOD Rd (1 sapper wounded)	
			1 section pushing up tramline for laying along the road	
	25/9/17		Baths	
	26/9/17		hutting	
	27/9/17		← ½ day	
	29/9/17		100 fascines for roads, hurdles made	
			Alterations to SCOTTISH WOOD camp to take Div H Q	
			No 46456 a/LCpl BLACKFORD awarded the military medal for bringing Sapr MAUNDER who was wounded & unable to walk out of a heavy shelled area on 24th	
	30/9/17		Sent huttg hub for Div H Q & taking charge of R.E. dump, No 3 section detached to actual dugouts for the M G Corps	
			MR Malcolm Major R.E. OC 97 Field Coy RE

Army Form C. 2118.

WAR DIARY
or
INTELLIGENCE SUMMARY.
(Erase heading not required.)

Instructions regarding War Diaries and Intelligence Summaries are contained in F. S. Regs., Part II. and the Staff Manual respectively. Title pages will be prepared in manuscript.

Place	Date	Hour	Summary of Events and Information	Remarks and references to Appendices
RIDGE WOOD	19/9/17		2 section work on tramway near YEOMANRY POST from 4.0 am till 11.0 am. 3 Sappers Wounded. 2 Section covered started work at SCOTTISH WOOD end but were stopped at 11.0 am afterwards paraded for work on the tramway at 4.0 pm	
	20/9/17		2 section paraded at 9.30 am & proceeded to lay tram light Railway from YEOMANRY POST to SANCTUARY WOOD they arrived there at 11.0 am and started work but had to wait until 11.30 am as the line was being shelled they then laid the railway to within 60' of the interest when they were relieved by the other section at 2.15 pm of which we were sent back as there were not enough for the job. The other section finished the line and made 150' of formation in the wood for a tramline extension & run of MANOR FARM.	
	21/9/17 22/9/17		All section working in SCOTTISH WOOD 1 Sapper Wounded by bomb from aeroplane	

21st

CONFIDENTIAL

WAR DIARY
OF
97th FIELD Co RE

1st – 31st Oct. 1917.

Vol 26

WAR DIARY or INTELLIGENCE SUMMARY

Army Form C. 2118.

Place	Date	Hour	Summary of Events and Information	Remarks and references to Appendices
RIDGE WOOD	1/10/17		No 1 supplied a small party & marched out the Div. Boundaries from the Canal to ZILLEBEKE LAKE. Nos 1,2 & 4 continued work on huts in SCOTTISH WOOD. No 3 section were killed with Pte 62nd 64th 110th & 237 M.G. Coys in GLENCORSE, POLYGON WOOD & CHATEAU WOOD on the way up the 64th party of 6 teams got detached & 4 missing (who in nineteen reported wounded badly the 110th party 2 became detached & the others were hit by a shell on the way & took to bring up stores from the BLACK WATCH Corner and an orderly. The trouble was that the Gunners started a running attack and they were caught in the barrage. The remainder of the party were taken by Pte & Lieutenant to man a support trench & they sheltered at a sheema, a German enemy aeroplane. They did no work that day Nos 1-4 went to lay their ideas arrived back in camp at 9.0 pm & went up again. 100 attached infantry joined the company.	
	2/10/17		10 of No 1 were sent up the dump 2 hrs later & joined went to GLENCORSE WOOD with them but were told to sleep. No 2 started on 4 shelters for Bde H.Q. W of STIRLING CASTLE. No 1 & 4 attached infantry continued work on camps & sent buggers Nissen huts for Div H.Q.	

Army Form C. 2118.

WAR DIARY
or
INTELLIGENCE SUMMARY.
(Erase heading not required.)

Place	Date	Hour	Summary of Events and Information	Remarks and references to Appendices
RIDGE WOOD	2/10/17	18	Notice boards were also completed	
		10	5 cappos at the dump were relieved by the 12th NF. Shell slits were completed for the 6th, 110th & 62nd MG Coy by No.3 Section. The 3 men sent had been worked with the 110th although placed in the 62nd.	
			mining & went to ambulance in the evening.	
			Party returned that evening having 3 men with the 237 who completed their shell slits next day & then returned.	
			No.2 Section. completed the R.E. Dump at GLENCORSE WOOD &	
			No.1 & 4 finished off Hdl 2a camp & to push aminals were to load	
			for practice with explosive materials	
			30 and much 40' long were much also shot not picked for	
	3/10/17		sharing were return the much the Signposts & notice boards were also made.	
			2. Parties limber wagons went up to GLENCORSE WOOD on arrival in the	
			wagon up & had to be left	

WAR DIARY
or
INTELLIGENCE SUMMARY.

(Erase heading not required.)

Army Form C. 2118.

Place	Date	Hour	Summary of Events and Information	Remarks and references to Appendices
RIDGE WOOD	4/10/17		12 hutments were made. 6 horse troughs found in an unauthorised place were removed to a rather lower level to say Ndl as troughs were allowed them, provide with the unit to which they belonged was enforced. 2 Pontoon wagons went up with stores to the N.E. bank at GLENCORSE WOOD & 8 pack animals to near CAMERON HOUSE. No1 recovered the empty hand wagon and carried a few stores forward but had to stop owing to a counter attack. Section continued work on SCOTTISH WOOD camp.	
	5/10/17		No3 & 4 section continued work on SCOTTISH WOOD camp	
	6/10/17		No1 the had the evening of the 2 Eastern handles of the POLYGON BECK. the there were not streams but boggy hollows and they much up the kerbes holes about 1½ roasts duck boards during so 50' in all. No2 uplaced 2 shelters at Belt Hd Qrs which had been blown up. No4 went up in the morning to do a ett material a recent enemy were down & to mend out the a post here.	

WAR DIARY
or
INTELLIGENCE SUMMARY.

Army Form C. 2118.

Place	Date	Hour	Summary of Events and Information	Remarks and references to Appendices
RIDGE WOOD	7/10/17		Lut 2d ROWE M.C. was wounded & Sgt. ? was delayed owing to having to take him till it was dark & had to give it up.	
			No 1 section duckboarded the track from POLYGONE BECK 120ˣ westwards near BELLS	
			No 4 were unable to get up owing to heavy shelling of the roads near WARDE LAKE which ? ? them	
			Nos 2 & 3 completed huts in SCOTTISH WOOD for Bde HQ	
	8/10/17		No 2 & 3 continued duckboarded the road & dublin track from J14.a.8.5. for 150ˣ laying them loose (1 Infantryman wounded , 1 ? but carried front shape)	
			No 1 & 4 carried a harrassing around the lower line	

Army Form C. 2118.

WAR DIARY
or
INTELLIGENCE SUMMARY.
(Erase heading not required.)

Instructions regarding War Diaries and Intelligence Summaries are contained in F. S. Regs. Part II. and the Staff Manual respectively. Title pages will be prepared in manuscript.

Place	Date	Hour	Summary of Events and Information	Remarks and references to Appendices
	9/10/17		The attached infantry regiments their Battalions to 1 section allied that for G.O.C. RA & worked on Scottish Wood Camp & Bart into a Company drying room. Nos 2, 3 & 4 completed shelters & bunk around Horse Shoe Camp	

Army Form C. 2118.

WAR DIARY
or
INTELLIGENCE SUMMARY.
(Erase heading not required.)

Instructions regarding War Diaries and Intelligence Summaries are contained in F. S. Regs., Part II. and the Staff Manual respectively. Title pages will be prepared in manuscript.

Place	Date	Hour	Summary of Events and Information	Remarks and references to Appendices
	10/10/17		" St Page & 6 men traced a track from J10C20 to J11C46 the remnants of No 1 found a shellproof track of 60 duckboards along the former Ypres-Poland road on GHEENGORSE WOOD TRACK Casualties 1 man slightly wounded but remained on duty.	
	11/10/17		The Coy moved to MILLEKRUISSE (N8a69 - sheet 28) and worked on their camp for the remainder of the day	
	12/10/17		No 1 & 3 commenced laying a platform of poles round the drinking troughs at Corps C.C.S. for horses, under C.R.E. X Corps Troops. Nos 2 & 4 commenced horse standings near camp also under C.R.E. X Corps Troops	
	13/10/17		Work continued as on 12/10/17	
	14/10/17		Baths & standards for horse standings carted to site	
	15/10/17		Work continued & horse standings at HALLEBAST CORNER commenced "U" T. E. MORGAN joined the Coy	
	16/10/17		Work continued "J" P. P. Page evacuated to C.C.S. Corduroy road renewed from horse lines at N.V.C.e.5. CUD ENDOOM completed	

WAR DIARY
INTELLIGENCE SUMMARY

Army Form C. 2118.

Place	Date	Hour	Summary of Events and Information	Remarks and references to Appendices
MULE TRVIS	19/10/17		HULLEBAST CORNER Shelter & all day. Heavy bombardment	
	20/10/17		Work continued	2nd Transport ready for routine
	21/10/17		Coy to work. 1 Man wounded by a bomb from an aeroplane	N 2 E 8.5 } Shelter all ranks evacuated & renewed flooring. No 2 b 6.4 } both due to damage while reinforced
	22/10/17		Marched to ELZENWALLE CHATEAU & made bivouac. 86 attached Infantry joined the Bn. L/Cpl TOTTENHAM was awarded the M. Military	
	23/10/17		Coys — for work on the 1/10/17 & 2/10/17 dissolved. No 1 & attached Infantry repaired the track from JARGON CROSS to POLYGONEVELT. Remainder worked on the camp & bivouac	
	24/10/17		No 2 & attached Infantry again repaired the track. No 3 & attached Infantry started a new track from HOOGE to GLENCORSE WOOD. Remainder worked in camp	
	25/10/17		No 1 & attached Infantry repaired the track & extended it 15ˣ (2 attached Infantry wounded). No 2 attached Infantry continued the new track	

Army Form C. 2118.

WAR DIARY
or
INTELLIGENCE SUMMARY.
(Erase heading not required.)

Place	Date	Hour	Summary of Events and Information	Remarks and references to Appendices
ELZEN WALLE CHATEAU	26/10/17		No 2 & attached infantry + No 4 & their attached infantry relieved the two [?] companies POLYGONEVELT & extended II Coy to the beginning of the dive run from HOOGE	
	27/10/17		No 3 carried up 40 hurd branch to the beginning of the dive run from HOOGE to a point 400 south of JARGON CROSS. No 4 & No 2 worked in cont.	
			No 1 & 2 ditto	
	29/10/17		ditto only action changed round	
			ditto	
			Exhaust pipe found to run in under at No4 H/Q HOOGE crater	
			& attached infantry	
			No 3 exhausted the duck pont POLYGONEVELT	
			No 2 repaired a rapid relay post 2 in GLENCORSE WOOD	
	30/10/17		Normal work resumed & one Sapper, major & in RE HQ (1 Sapper & 2 infantry wounded chamois complete)	
	31/10/17		Work continued. Track from POLYGONEVELT taken to J.9 b 8.9 the track to JARGON CROSS completed & duckboards fixed for half its length. The engine connected up till the majority to work to run	

O.C. 27 Coy R.E / Major RE

C.R.E.
41st Div.

Works Report No 3 Section

1st just acted as Infantry

2nd Cleaned out 2 MEBUS in POLYGON WOOD at J9 d.1.

3rd Cleaned out one MEBU at V9 d.0.0. due 16 shell slits for 110th Bde. M.G.Coy. & partly covered ones for Battery Commanders. Dimensions 5' x 2' x 5' deep

Also 8 similar slits for 62 M.G.Coy. The 64th Coy. R.A. doing their own work and Cpl Mason is still with the 237th Coy whom he will leave with his 2 men on completion.

Shell slits were unstarted

3/10/17
W Wilson Major R.E.
O.C. 97th C.T.

WAR DIARY
or
INTELLIGENCE SUMMARY
(Erase heading not required.)

Army Form C. 2118.

97th Field Coy R.E.

Vol 27

Place	Date	Hour	Summary of Events and Information	Remarks and references to Appendices
ELZENWALLE CHATEAU	1/11/17		POLYGONNE VELT track extended & existing track repaired & new track from HOOGE completed by Nos 1.3.&4 sections. No 2 section & attached infantry work in camp.	
"	2/11/17		Work on POLYGONNE VELT continued by Nos 1.2.&4 sections & attached infantry. No 3 section & infantry work in camp.	
"	3/11/17		Work on tracks continued by Nos 1.2. &3 sections & attached infy. but much hindered by hostile shelling. No 4 section & infy in camp.	
"	4/11/17		POLYGONNE VELT track taken past turning to BUTTE. Nos 3 section & infy in camp. Also Nos 2 & 4 sections & infy work on track. No 3 section & infy in camp. Installed motor pump HOOGE CRATER.	
"	5/11/17		Tracks worked on by Nos 1 & 3 sections & attached infy. Nos 2 & 4 sects & attached infy work in camp.	
"	6/11/17		Nos 2 & 4 section & attached infantry worked on tracks. One sapper wounded. Nos 1 & 3 section & attached infantry work in camp.	
"	7/11/17		Nos 1, 2, &3 section & attached infantry work on tracks, No 4 r infy in camp.	

Army Form C. 2118.

WAR DIARY
or
INTELLIGENCE SUMMARY.
(Erase heading not required.)

Instructions regarding War Diaries and Intelligence Summaries are contained in F. S. Regs., Part II. and the Staff Manual respectively. Title pages will be prepared in manuscript.

Place	Date	Hour	Summary of Events and Information	Remarks and references to Appendices
ECZEN-WALLE CHATEAU	8/11/17		Work on Tracks by Nos 1, 3, & 4 Sections & attached infantry. No 2 Section & attached infantry walk in camp	
"	9/11/17		Track Completed to within 25 yards of by Nos 2, 3, & 4 Section & attached infantry. No 1 attached infantry walk in Camp.	
"	10/11/17		No 1 Section work in camp at ZILLEBEKE. No 3 Section work on C.R.E. dump. Queens work at LA CLYTTE dump. No 2 & 4 Section with attached infantry and 1/2 H.Qrs & Divisional baths	
"	11/11/17		No 1 Section work at ZILLEBEKE. No 2 & Infy work at Div HQrs. No 3 Section work at Dump. No 4 Section & Infy work on horse lines near Div. H.Qrs. Queens work at LA CLYTTE dump	
"	12/11/17		Same as 11/11/17	
"	13/11/17		Nos 1 & 3 Section bathed & then worked as 11/11/17. No 2 Section with inf(?) as 11/11/17 & also work Belong aeroplane DICKEBUSCH LAKE. No 4 Section & Infy work as 11/11/17	

Army Form C. 2118.

WAR DIARY
or
INTELLIGENCE SUMMARY.
(Erase heading not required.)

Instructions regarding War Diaries and Intelligence Summaries are contained in F. S. Regs., Part II. and the Staff Manual respectively. Title pages will be prepared in manuscript.

Place	Date	Hour	Summary of Events and Information	Remarks and references to Appendices
ELZENWALLE	14/4/17		No 2 Section completed work on barrage of aeroplanes at MICKELBURGH LAKE. No 1.3, & 4 Sections holiday. Attached Infantry	
CHATEAU			return to units 2.30 pm.	
WESTOUTRE	15/4/17		Company moved to CONQUEROR CAMP WESTOUTRE arriving 10.30 pm.	
"	16/4/17		Company rested.	
BOULIEU	17/4/17		Company march off 9 am. arrived BOULIEU (L.10.b.6.8. Sheet 36) at 2.30 pm.	
GONNEHEM	18/4/17	10 am.	" " " GONNEHEM 10pm	
COUPIGNY	19/4/17	8 am.	" " " COUPIGNY 1.30 5pm	
St ELOY	20/4/17	10.25 am.	" " " OTTAWA CAMP, Mt. ST ELOY at 1.45 pm.	
ECURIE AREA	21/4/17	9.45 am.	" " " G.3.d.2.2. Sheet 57B at 12 noon	
"	22/4/17		Company rested. Officers N.C.O.s & No 2 Sec. sections inspected work on communicating trenches under C.R.E. 31st Div Orders	

WAR DIARY
or
INTELLIGENCE SUMMARY

Army Form C. 2118.

Place	Date	Hour	Summary of Events and Information	Remarks and references to Appendices
3d.a.a. Sht 51B	22/4/19		Nos 2 & 4 Sections with 200 men of 3/4 Queens work on OISE & TONY allege. Nos 1 & 3 in Camp.	
"	24/4/19		Nos 2 & 4 Sections & Infantry continue work on Trenches. Nos 1 & 3 in Camp.	
"	25/4/19		All Sections in Camp. Drill, training, & work in Camp etc. Lt T. McPhee joined.	
"	26/4/19		Company fatted. Drill etc.	
"	27/4/19		No 2 Section during the forenoon still dump. Remainder Drill & Training	
"	28/4/19		In Camp. Training etc	
"	29/4/19		" " . 1 gnr Meeks totd by Cape KIRK.	
"	30/4/19		Training etc Harness inspection. Company moved, dismounted left camp 11.45 entrained MAROEUIL, detrained marched off 9.30pm Capt LOWE returned. Disembarked left MAROEUIL at 5.0 am	

W.G.Dunn
Major RE
O.C. 97 Coy RE

Army Form C. 2118.

WAR DIARY
or
INTELLIGENCE SUMMARY.
(Erase heading not required.)

917th Field by RE
Dec 1917

Place	Date	Hour	Summary of Events and Information	Remarks and references to Appendices
ÉCURIE MAROEUIL Station	1/12/17		Entrained at MAROEUIL at 5.0 a.m. the transport holted at BRAUME Company detrained at PERONNE at 1.30 p.m. & marched to BRUSLE at 4.0 p.m. the transport at 7.0 p.m. Put up temporary shelters for our Artillery at BRUSLE	
BRUSLE	2/12/17		ditto	
"	3/12/17			
"	4/12/17		Dismounted parties marched to EPEHY & clay 4 strong points at E N W end of village & also garrisoning them one officer & two [?] on the 7th at the SE end of village taken of every supper Supervision of 4 works at TINCOURT ½ by [?] at TINCOURT	
	7/12/17 8/12/17			
	9/12/17 10/12/17			
	11/12/17		a new work started on NE face of village Parts removed from 60 m hill g[?] elms	
	12/12/17 13/12/17 14/12/17		ditto Capt Fraser RE arrived	
	15/12/17		The engineered parts at the SE end of the village started a new fort to the [?] on the [?] a new side ditto Capt V [Gaur?] left before the fort broken [?]	

Army Form C. 2118.

WAR DIARY
or
INTELLIGENCE SUMMARY.
(Erase heading not required.)

Instructions regarding War Diaries and Intelligence Summaries are contained in F. S. Regs., Part II. and the Staff Manual respectively. Title pages will be prepared in manuscript.

Place	Date	Hour	Summary of Events and Information	Remarks and references to Appendices
EPÉHY	19/12/17		Work on huts continued	
	20/12/17		" " " "	
	21/12/17		Nos 2 & 4 sections moved to LIERAMONT and slept in huts & started M.H & event	
LIERAMONT	22/12/17		Coy HQ moved to LIERAMONT	
	23/12/17		No 1 & 3 huts huts. Transport moved 2.30 pm X mas dinner 2.30 km at LIERAMONT	
	24/12/17		Work continued	
	25/12/17		Work ceased at 9.30 am Xmas dinner 2.30 pm at LIERAMONT	
	26/12/17		Work continued	
	27/12/17		" "	
	30/12/17			
	31/12/17		Work continued work on huts started	

W.M. Major R.E.
OC 97" Coy R.E.

21st Div.

WAR DIARY

97th FIELD COMPANY, R.E.

M A R C H

(1/23.3.18)

1 9 1 8

Army Form C. 2118.

WAR DIARY
or
INTELLIGENCE SUMMARY.
(Erase heading not required.)

Instructions regarding War Diaries and Intelligence Summaries are contained in F. S. Regs., Part II. and the Staff Manual respectively. Title pages will be prepared in manuscript.

Place	Date	Hour	Summary of Events and Information	Remarks and references to Appendices
IERAMONT	18		Work continued on dug-outs by batted.	
"	19		Section of Bde. H.Q. dug-out. In Bn Artillery	
"	20		Commenced at W.21.c.1.4. Work on all dug-outs ceased owing to order "Stand to" being received	
			Total elevations on all dug-outs Shelters from hits of dug-outs which were ready 1976-6" (13 large opening No 3)	Heavy shell fire infantry men worked
			H.Q. No 1 & 3 Section LIERAMONT. No 2 Section W.20.b.5.3. H.Q. Section	
"	21		W.15.a.5.4 HEUDECOURT.	
			Intense enemy bombardment opened on our lines at 3.30 am	
			Nos 1 & 3 Sections stood to in LIERAMONT defences	
			No 4 Section stood to in Sunken Road W.21.c.1.4. close & Coy H.Q. at HAM. and at 5 am were ordered by Lieut TOTTENHAM Brigade to Coy H.Q.	
			No 2 Section with 50 attached Infantry under Lt. G. Goodenoughkins and 2nd Lieutn	
			Hunt Knighton stood to in trench at W.15 a 9.3 in front of HEUDECOURT in heavy barrage, nearly 80× perimeter every	
			if heavy gas shower from gas shells. During this bombardment 9 Sappers	
			and 3 attached Infantrymen were killed and 3 Sappers and 1 Infantry Sergeant wounded by Shell fire. At 5-30 am the Section received orders to report at Coy H.Q. The Section failed out in parties of 4.	

WAR DIARY or INTELLIGENCE SUMMARY

Army Form C. 2118.

Place	Date	Hour	Summary of Events and Information	Remarks and references to Appendices
	21		and arrived at Coy H.Q. LIERAMONT at 10 am. & twenty four dent and wounded men to the Dressing Station. without further casualties.	
			The party were Box Respirators for C Section as having gas cloud and had no casualties from gas, all men being able to wear the Small Box.	
			At 11 p.m. orders were received from the C.R.E. for dismounted portion of Coy to report to O.C. 110th S.B. at SAULCOURT and to proceed to dig & hold a trench if required, leaving a reasonable person in charge of the Coy Transport. Lt Houston-McLean was left in charge of the Coy Transport and the Coy under Capt N.F.C. Freeman and Lieuts Dalzyer & Tettenham & Lieut Morgan proceeded once tent valleys were arranged to dig and hold a trench about E.11.c. The Coy worked on the trench during the night.	
	2		The trench which the Coy were holding ran 6th December was heavily shelled at 7 am. the bombardment lasting for an hour and a half.	

WAR DIARY or INTELLIGENCE SUMMARY

Army Form C. 2118.

Place	Date	Hour	Summary of Events and Information	Remarks and references to Appendices
	2.		as the men were ordered to leave the trench were taken up as hostages in shell holes in front of the trench. Lieut. Q.L. Allyno was wounded when leaving the trench. About 11 am the position was being surrounded by the enemy and the C.O. & 6th Lincolns ordered the garrison of York Trench. The withdrawal was then carried out under M.G. fire and most of the Coy were seen being surrounded & cut off by the enemy, only Lieut Allyno, 1 Sergeant & 6 O.R. being able to get clear. During the morning the three of 126th Field Coy R.E. were ordered to the H.Q. of this Coy at LIERAMONT. Orders were received from C.R.E. for all attached Infantry to report at 73 Bde. H.Q. HEUDECOURT. The party under Lieut. Kingston, 2nd Lincolns moved off at 1.30 hrs. LIERAMONT and vicinity of Coy H.Q. being shelled by the enemy the transport moved off through AIZE COURT LE BAS	

WAR DIARY
or
INTELLIGENCE SUMMARY

Place	Date	Hour	Summary of Events and Information	Remarks and references to Appendices
	22		while the transport was moving the convoy was shelled and several of the mules were hit. 12 E.A flight bn attacked the column with M.G. fire and every opportunity was afforded to the rifle party on them & succeeded in driving them off. Transfer of the Coy arrived at HAUT ALLAINES 11.45 p.m & camped. Orders were received the for transfer of mules to 62nd F.B. Servicer of the Coy's attached infantry afforded H.R.	
	23		The Coy moved at 4.30 a.m and arrived at CLERY-SUR-SOMME at 2 p.m and camped. All stores for demolitions were handed over to a R.E. officer of 39th Div. F. for immediate use. Order received from C.R.E. that we are all to parade near the Cookhouse next to report to Major Marsden R.E. of 12 Field Coy R.E. for duty. Order received from C.R.E. about 3.30 p.m. regarding 97, 98, 5/126 th Field Coy's R.E. to be amalgamated into 1 Coy to be known as 31st Div't Coy R.E.	

Edwin Biggs Capt
W. Isham Major R.E.
O.C. 97th Coy R.E.

21st Divisional Engineers

97th FIELD COMPANY R.E. :::: APRIL 1918.

Army Form C. 2118.

WAR DIARY
or
INTELLIGENCE SUMMARY.
(Erase heading not required.)

91st Field Coy RE
Vol 3

Place	Date	Hour	Summary of Events and Information	Remarks and references to Appendices
HANGEST SUR SOMME	1/4/18		Company entrained at HANGEST-SUR-SOMME at 6.30 p.m.	
	2/4		Company detrained at PESEL HOEK at 7.30 a.m. and proceeded to LOCRE in motor lorries	
LOCRE	3/4		Company rested	
	4/4		Company marched to R.E. farm	
R.E. FARM	5/4		Company worked in Camp	
"	6/4		Work in Camp continued	
"	7/4		" "	
"	8/4		Company bathed	
"	9/4		Work in Camp continued after marching order inspection	
"	10/4		Company marched to CHATEAU SEGARD (H.30.c.5.5). Work taken over from 456" 3rd Coy R.E. — Officers MCOs & mounted Corps line posts	
CHATEAU SEGARD	11/4		70 attached infantry joined Company. Work on posts commenced	

WAR DIARY or INTELLIGENCE SUMMARY

Army Form C. 2118.

Place	Date	Hour	Summary of Events and Information	Remarks and references to Appendices
CHATEAU SEGARD	12/4/18		Work on posts continued. 250 x 4 inch 3" dump holes of MENIN ROAD. Bridges across YPRES-COMINES CANAL between KRUISSTRAATHOEK - YPRES and SHRAPNEL CORNER - WYTSCHAETE roads, including reconnected with a view to demolition.	
	13/4		Work on posts continued. Charges for demolition of bridges across YPRES COMINES CANAL prepared. Preparation of bridges for demolition commenced in evening.	
	14/4		Work on posts & demolitions continued.	
	15/4		" " " " Company prepared to march off. 6 p.m. Order cancelled by C.R.E.	
	16/4		Company marched to OUDERDOM (BOWNSIDE CAMP) 89 reinforcements joined company.	
OUDERDOM	17/4		Nos 1+2 Sections worked on G.H.Q. line. No 3+4 Section worked	

Army Form C. 2118.

WAR DIARY
or
INTELLIGENCE SUMMARY.
(Erase heading not required.)

Instructions regarding War Diaries and Intelligence Summaries are contained in F. S. Regs., Part II. and the Staff Manual respectively. Title pages will be prepared in manuscript.

Place	Date	Hour	Summary of Events and Information	Remarks and references to Appendices
OUDERDOM	18/4		at Bde H.Q. meeting Shelters. "2/Lt E. CLOUGH) " " H.H. ALLEN) Joined company. " " A.G. BOOTH)	
"	19/4		Work at Bde H.Q., on G.H.Q. line and BRASSERIE continued. 900x wire erected round VOORMEZEELE. Breastwork & knife rests at ELZENWALLE dump. Work at Bde H.Q. Continued. 2/Lt A.G. BOOTH wounded.	
"	20/4		Work continued as 19/4/16.	
"	21/4		2/Lt G. BOOTES joined company. N°4 Section Continued work on Bde H.Q. Remainder continued work on BRASSERIE, G.H.Q. line and M.G. emplacements in VOORMEZEELE.	

Army Form C. 2118.

WAR DIARY
or
INTELLIGENCE SUMMARY
(Erase heading not required.)

Instructions regarding War Diaries and Intelligence Summaries are contained in F. S. Regs., Part II. and the Staff Manual respectively. Title pages will be prepared in manuscript.

Place	Date	Hour	Summary of Events and Information	Remarks and references to Appendices
OUDERDOM	22/4/18		Nos 1, 2 and 4 and 1st Lincs. Continued work. No 3 and 12/13 N.F. commenced work on VOORMEZEELE - KRUISSTRAATHOEK switch. Lt G.G. MCLEAN, 1 sapper and 3 attached infantry (1st Lincs) wounded	
"	23/4		1/2 company bathed. 1/2 company continued work	
"	24/4			
"	25/4		Work postponed owing to enemy attack. Company moved to farm North West of OUDERDOM (G.24.b.3.3.)	
OUDERDOM (G.24.b.33)	26/4		Lt J.D. FETTES joined company. Nos 1, 2, & 3 sections worked at night. Cutting trench & erecting headworks across BRASSERIE - ELZEN WALLE road and at ELZEN WALLE DUMP. No 4 section worked by day at Bde H.Q.	
"	27/4		No 4 section continued work at Bde H.Q. Remainder of sections continued work at night blocking road in G.H.Q. line Major J.T. FISHER wounded	

Army Form C. 2118.

WAR DIARY
or
INTELLIGENCE SUMMARY

(Erase heading not required.)

Place	Date	Hour	Summary of Events and Information	Remarks and references to Appendices
OUDERDOM (G.24.b.3.5)	29/4/18		No 4 Section worked at Bde H.Q. Remainder worked at night as on 27/4/18.	
"	29/4/18		All sections attached infantry worked at night repairing wire & trenches East of RIDGE WOOD. 2 attached infantry (1st Lincs) killed. 1 R.E. wounded. No 2 N.E.'s missing at Bde H.Q. Remainder of company	
"	30/4		No 4 Section worked at Bde H.Q. Remainder worked at night as on 29/4/18.	

M.W.Collyns
Lt. R.E.
A/OC. 97 Coy R.E.

WAR DIARY
of
INTELLIGENCE SUMMARY.
(Erase heading not required.)

Army Form C. 2118.

97. Field Coy.
May 1918

Place	Date	Hour	Summary of Events and Information	Remarks and references to Appendices
OUDERDOM	1.5.18	4.0 pm	Company marched to form Area one mile S.E. of POPERINGHE	
POPERINGHE	2		do. a wood 1½ miles East of STEENVOORDE and bivouaced	
STEENVOORDE	3		do. a field ¼ mile East of LEDERZEELE and bivouaced	
LEDERZEELE	4		do. and entrained at ARQUES	
ON RAIL	5		Company travelling by rail	
SERZY SAVIGNY	6		do. detrained at SAVIGNY STATION and marched to ANTHENAY	
ANTHENAY	7		Company paraded and included 10.0 am.; Arm Drill 10.30 to 11.30. Physical Drill 12 noon – 12.45 pm.	
do.	8		Bathing parades Ft Company by sections 9.15 am. to 4.0 pm. Sections exercised in Drill and Physical Training.	
do.	9		No. 1, 2 & 3 Sections exercised in Arm Drill, Close Order Drill etc. 9.0 am to 1.0pm. No. 4 Section employed dis-infecting stables. Horses inspection 3.35pm.	
do.	10		Company exercised in Arm Drill and Physical Training. Inspection of Tents.	
do.	11		do. of Foot Gear.	
do.	12	3.0pm	Company moved to LHERY	

Army Form C. 2118.

WAR DIARY
or
INTELLIGENCE SUMMARY.
(Erase heading not required.)

Instructions regarding War Diaries and Intelligence Summaries are contained in F.S. Regs., Part II. and the Staff Manual respectively. Title pages will be prepared in manuscript.

Place	Date	Hour	Summary of Events and Information	Remarks and references to Appendices
	MAY			
LHERY	13		Company moved to PROUILLY	
PROUILLY	14		Company moved to CHALONS LE VERGUER. No 2 Section going to forward billets at CORMICY.	
CHALONS LE VERGUER	15		Company in Camp. No 4 Section proceeded to CORMICY. 11th F.S. KINGSTON with 100 attached Infantry joined the Company.	
do.	16		No 1 Section worked on Div. H.Q. Camp and O.P. at FONTAINE ST AUBŒUF. No 2 " " wiring trench north of LA NEUVILLE. " 3 " " proceeded to CORMICY. " 4 " " in Camp. Attached Infantry in Camp.	
do.	17		No 1 Section worked on Div. H.Q. Camp and O.P. at FONTAINE ST AUBŒUF. " 2 " " bored shaft north of LA NEUVILLE " 3 " " worked on Pireotho in Platoon Post at junction of STEPHANIE BOYAU and TRANCHEE de MITTAU " 4 " " moved to MADLON near MOSCOW and with attached Infantry party carried augerholes & cut &c sand shield bored Pireotho near left Battn. H.Q. of N.F.'s moved in quarters at CORMICY placed to M. 4 Section attached party	

Army Form C. 2118.

WAR DIARY
or
INTELLIGENCE SUMMARY.
(Erase heading not required.)

Place	Date	Hour	Summary of Events and Information	Remarks and references to Appendices
CHALONS LE VERGUER	MAY 18		No.1 Section with attached party 1st Divn. continued work on O.P. and New Brigade H.Q. at FONTAINE ST. AUBOEUF	
			" 2 Section continued wiring march north of LA NEUVILLE and screening the ROUTE NATIONALE No. 44 [LAON-REIMS Road] near ECLUSE D'ALGER	
			" 3 Section worked on Loopholes in Posts in TRANCHEE DE MITTAU.	
			" 4 " revetted Firesteps near Left Battn. H.Q.	
	19		No.1 Section continued work on O.P. and New Brigade H.Q. at FONTAINE ST. AUBOEUF	
			" 2 " wiring march north of LA NEUVILLE; also erected 125 yards 17 strand on LAON-REIMS Road north of ECLUSE D'ALGER.	
			" 3 Section completed Loopholes of 3 Platoon Posts in TR. DE MITTAU.	
			" 4 " revetted & improved Hearths near Left Battn. H.Q. and re-directed Camouflage at Moscow.	
	20		No.1 Section continued work on O.P. and new Brigade H.Q. at FONTAINE ST AUBOEUF	
			" 2 " erected 400 yards Apron Wire Fence in march N. of LA NEUVILLE and 110 yards of Screening along the LAON-REIMS Road.	
			" 3 Section made 65 yards Firesteps in Platoon Posts in TR. DE MITTAU	
			" 4 " continued work on Firesteps in sector of Left Battn.; also on Notice Boards.	

WAR DIARY or INTELLIGENCE SUMMARY

Army Form C. 2118.

Place	Date	Hour	Summary of Events and Information	Remarks and references to Appendices
CHALONS LE VERGUER	MAY 21		No. 1 Section continued work at FONTAINE ST AUBOEUF	
			" 2 " erected 200 yards of Screening on LAON-RHEIMS Road in rear of Brigade Boundary.	
			" 3 Section made 53 yards of Trestep in Posts BRYAU GUNNEMER and ECLUSE SUD	
			" 4 Section worked on 7 Trestep in Post near Left Batt'n H.Q., repaired 500 yards French tram track and painted sign-boards.	
	22		No. 1 Section continued work at FNE ST AUBOEUF	
			" 2 " erected 170 yards of Screen along LAON-RHEIMS Road	
			" 3 " Completed Trestep in Right Platoon Posts on the line of RESISTANCE N.E. of LAON-RHEIMS Road	
			" 4 Section continued Trestep in Platoon posts on MAIN LINE of RESISTANCE in Left Batt'n Area, also on Notice Boards.	
	23		No. 1 Section continued work at FNE ST AUBOEUF. Commenced Bath at Div. H.Q. CHALONS LE VERGUER. Made Alidades for Div Artillery	
			" 2 Section erected 70 yards of Screen on LAON-RHEIMS Rd.	
			" 3 " made 6½ yards Trestep in Platoon Posts on Main Line of Resistance	
			" 4 " Left Batt'n Sect. 1 Main Line of Resist'ce, cleared 30 yards of BRYAU DE RUTH H.Q. W. of MOISY and made Notice Boards.	

Army Form C. 2118.

WAR DIARY
or
INTELLIGENCE SUMMARY.

Place	Date	Hour	Summary of Events and Information	Remarks and references to Appendices
AISNE LE VERGUER	MAY 24		No 1 Section continued work at ST AUBOEUF and Bath at Div H.Q.	
			" 2 " erected 80 yards of Screen along LAON-RHEIMS Road	
			" 3 " Continued Firesteps & Platoon Posts in Premier & Resist Co in Right Battn Area and commenced erection of Trench Gates	
			" 4 Section continued Firesteps & Platoon Posts in Premier & Resist Co in Left Battn Area and cleared 35 yards of BOYAU DE BUTE 144. W. of MOSCOU.	
"	25		No 1 Section continued work at FNE ST AUBOEUF and Bath at Div H.Q.	
			" 2 " Erected 100 yards of Screen on LAON-RHEIMS Road	
			" 3 " Continued to make Firesteps as yesterday, also making and erecting Trench Gates.	
			" 4 Section continued Firesteps as yesterday; cleared 30 yards of BOYAU ST. ALICE, making Trench Gates, making and painting Notice Boards.	
"	26		No 1 Section continued work on FNE ST. AUBOEUF and Bath at Div. H.Q.	
			" 2 " erected 90 yards of Screen on LAON-RHEIMS Road	
			" 3 " making and erecting Trench Gates	
			" 4 " Continued making Firesteps in Boyau de la MARINE, clearing 25 yards of BOYAU ST. ALICE and making Trench Gates. No. 4 Section withdrawn from Moscou about midnight 26-27th	

Army Form C. 2118.

WAR DIARY
or
INTELLIGENCE SUMMARY.

(Erase heading not required.)

Place	Date	Hour	Summary of Events and Information	Remarks and references to Appendices
CHALONS LE VERGUER	MAY 27		German attack commenced about 1.0 a.m. Camp lightly shelled but suffered from fire and tanks were both between 2.0 and 5.0 a.m. No. 2 & 3 Sections withdrew from CORMICY and reached H.Q. of Company between 10.30 a.m. and 12.30 p.m., having passed through a heavy enemy barrage (One Sapper killed, two wounded). The Sections and attached Infantry, commanded by Capt. R.H. COLLYNS R.E. left under orders to report to 110th Inf. Bde. and thereafter came under the orders of the 64th Inf. Bde. and were attached first with 15th D.L.I. in holding the line of the light Railway West of CAUROY. The Transport under Lieut. J.D. FETTES R.E. & 2/Lt CHALLIS LE VERGUER & 2/Lt BOUVANCOURT arriving at 6.07 p.m. The Road was under fire from M.G. or E.A. and from occasional shrapnel bursts.	
BRANSCOURT	28		Transport moved from TOWER CAMP to a Camp N. of BRANSCOURT arriving about 3.0 a.m. and rested till 9.30 a.m. Then proceeded to VILLE EN TARDENOIS where it was joined in the evening by the Transport of 98 Fd. Coy R.E. 2/Lieut. H.H. ALLEN R.E. slightly wounded while passing off TRIGNY.	

WAR DIARY
or
INTELLIGENCE SUMMARY

Army Form C. 2118.

Place	Date	Hour	Summary of Events and Information	Remarks and references to Appendices
VILLE EN TARDENOIS	MAY 29		The Transport in company with the Transport of the 126 Rd. Bty. (which had merged from LHERY) and of the 98 Rd. Bty. marched to MARFAUX and bivouaced. Capt. R.H. COLLYNS R.E. severely wounded while retiring main line of Railway at MUIZON on the VESLE RIVER.	
MARFAUX	30		The Transport along with the Officers Servers and attached Infantry who had returned from the Line, marched with the 98 + 126 Rd. Btys to the Forest D'EPERNAY and camped at the Southern edge of the Clearing on the VAUCIENNES — ST MARTIN D'ABLOIS Road about one mile N. of the latter place. Bridging equipment unloaded at DAMERY Pt Cornot-station. Bridge troops the MARNE RIVER by the 62nd Inf. Bde and The Company came under the Orders of that Bde. and marched to SOULIERES, arriving at 4.0 p.m.	
FOREST D'EPERNAY	31			
SOULIERES	JUNE 1		Company rested at SOULIERES. Two lectures on Tent Cart moved to join the Divisional Composite Force, the Mounted min. Sutursung at VILLERS aux BOIS and the Transport morning to CHALTRAIT.	

WAR DIARY
or
INTELLIGENCE SUMMARY

Army Form C. 2118.

97th Field Coy R.E.

VIII 34

June 1918

Place	Date	Hour	Summary of Events and Information	Remarks
SOULIERES	JUNE 1		Company rested at SOULIERES. No 2 and 4 Sections, under Lieut. BOOTES and LIEUT. CARNELLEY respectively, and complete with Transport less 1 Tool Cart, moved to join the Divisional Composite Force; the dismounted men entraining at VILLERS aux BOIS and the Transport moving to CHALTRAIT.	
"	2		Bdr Reopened inspection and drill for Company. Attached Infantry. Company (less 2 Sections) and Attached Infantry bathed at Pit battery shown in village.	
"	3		(less 2 Sections) Company marched with 126 Coy R.E. to VILLEVENARD and 62nd Infantry Brigade to VILLEVENARD and camped with posts of 126 Coy RE about ½ mile NNW of the village, arriving about 2.15 p.m.	
VILLEVENARD	4		Company (less 2 Sections) and Attached Infantry paraded 9.30 a.m. No 3 Section worked weapons. Harness inspection. Attacked Infantry (under Lieut. KINGSTON took 63 Other Ranks) reported to their respective Battalions. Company moved to billets in the village of VILLEVENARD.	

WAR DIARY or INTELLIGENCE SUMMARY

Army Form C. 2118.

Place	Date	Hour	Summary of Events and Information	Remarks and references to Appendices
VILLEVENARD	JUNE 5		Company less 2 sections. Lectures Parade. 9.0 am. Parade. Lecture Drill 9.15 am. – 10.15 am. Box Respirator drill 10.45 am. to 11.15 am. Musketry Drill 11.30 am. – 12.0 pm. Physical drill 12.15 pm. – 12.45 pm. Mounted Section – Box Respirator drill, Mounted Stable duties.	
"	6		9.0 am. – 12.45 pm. Tactical Exercise for Sections 1 and 3. Demolition of Stone Arch Bridge and wooden bridge across the PETIT MORIN which runs westward about 1000 yards south of VILLEVENARD – assuming that the Enemy was marching Northwards.	
"	7		No. 1 and 3 Sections parade 9.6 am. 9.15 – 11.30 am. Musketry (including the firing of 5 rounds by each man at Bull's-eye Targets). 11.45 am. to 12.15 pm. Box Respirator drill 12.15 pm. – 12.45 pm Physical Training. Inspection by Divisional pro H.C.O. of all Box Respirators in the Company.	

Army Form C. 2118.

WAR DIARY
or
INTELLIGENCE SUMMARY.
(Erase heading not required.)

Instructions regarding War Diaries and Intelligence Summaries are contained in F. S. Regs., Part II. and the Staff Manual respectively. Title pages will be prepared in manuscript.

Place	Date	Hour	Summary of Events and Information	Remarks and references to Appendices
VILLEVENARD	JUNE 8	9.0 am to 12.45 pm	Tactical Exercise for Sections 1 and 3. Construction of two bridges across the PETIT MORIN which were destroyed about 1000 yards south of VILLEVENARD — assuming that the enemy was retreating northwards.	
	9		No. 1 Section with one detail of No. 2 Section (working with 2 H/9s. a total of 25.) present with 40 men of 98 Fd.Cy.RE under Capt. WEDGWOOD RE (126 Fd.Ct.) and LIEUT MCLAREN RE (98 Fd.Ct.) proceeded by Busses at 8.0 am. to join the Divisional Cyclist Coy RE at IGNY-LE-JARD. The Company (less 3 Sections) with details and part Transport of 126 Fd. Cy attached, marched with 62nd Infantry Brigade to the village BEAUVAIS LA MODE (about 5 miles west of SEZANNE) and billeted.	

Army Form C. 2118.

WAR DIARY
or
INTELLIGENCE SUMMARY.
(Erase heading not required.)

Instructions regarding War Diaries and Intelligence Summaries are contained in F. S. Regs., Part II. and the Staff Manual respectively. Title pages will be prepared in manuscript.

Place	Date	Hour	Summary of Events and Information	Remarks and references to Appendices
BEAUVAIS LA NOUE	JUNE 10		No 3 Section and attached dismounts men of 126 Coy RE paraded 10.0 am and were instructed in Musketry, Box respirator and Physical Training. Company bathed in stream between BEAUVAIS and LA NOUE	
"	11		No. 3 Section and attached dismounted men of 126 Coy RE paraded 9.0 am and were instructed in Musketry and Box Respirator till 11.0 am. bathed troops afterwards. Mounted Section both Coys instructed in Box respirator	
"	12		No. 3 Section. Tactical Exercise. Defence of Village of BEAUVAIS on the assumption that Enemy is marching northwards.	
"	13		Company and attached details 126 Coy Box respirators inspected by Company Gas NCO. No 3 Section paraded 9.0 am. Lecture by Lieut CLOUGH on Results of yesterday's Tactical Exercise combined with such Reading	
"	14		No 3 Section paraded 9.0 am were instructed in Musketry from Drill till 11.0 am. One NCO. of each Coy reported to Intraining Officer at SEZANNE at 1.0 pm and proceeded by first train to LONGPRÉ to Advance party. Company (less 3 Section) with details and part Transport of 126 Coy RE attached paraded 9.55 pm to SEZANNE Station. Arrived 12.0 midnight. Bivouaced in Station Yard.	

WAR DIARY
or
INTELLIGENCE SUMMARY.

(Erase heading not required.)

Army Form C. 2118.

Instructions regarding War Diaries and Intelligence Summaries are contained in F.S. Regs., Part II. and the Staff Manual respectively. Title pages will be prepared in manuscript.

Place	Date	Hour	Summary of Events and Information	Remarks and references to Appendices
SEZANNE	JUNE 15		Company (less 3 sections) with details and part Transport of 126 Fd Co. attached. Entrained 7.30 am. Left 10.30 am. Passed by Rest and North side of PARIS between 5.0 am and 7.0 pm.	
HALLENCOURT	16		Company (less 3 sections) with details and part Transport of 126 Fd Co. attached detrained at LONGPRE 7.30 a.m. and breakfasted. Dismounted men journeyed by Motor lorries to HALLENCOURT arrived 11.0 am. Transport marched to HALLENCOURT, arrived 11.0 am. Billeted in village.	
ST AUBIN RIVIERE	17		Company (less 3 sections) with details and part Transport of 126 Fd Co. attached marched 11.15 am. with 62nd Brigade. Company details as ante. arrived ST. AUBIN RIVIERE 5:30 pm. and billeted.	
"	18		No.3 Section and attached men of 126 Fd Co. paraded 9.0 am. After inspection washed and cleaned wagons. Mounted Section and NCOs dismounted inspection 8.30 am. Lieut ALLEN rejoined Coy. from Hospital. Lieut de MAINE joined as Reinforcement. Lieut SKINNER and Lieut MOLONEY joined as Reinforcement for 126 Fd Co. RE.	

Army Form C. 2118.

WAR DIARY
or
INTELLIGENCE SUMMARY.
(Erase heading not required.)

Place	Date	Hour	Summary of Events and Information	Remarks and references to Appendices
ST AUBIN RIVIERE	JUNE 19		No 3 Section paraded 9.0 am. and were instructed in Musketry. Firing on range. Box respirators and Physical Training till 12.45 pm. H.Q. Lewis Gunners commenced instruction in Lewis Gun. 9/4 men per Section. Mounted Section paraded 8.30 am. An inspection of Iron Ration. Lieut CARNELLEY and 1st Lieut BOOTES with Sections 1, 2 and 4 returned 10.30 pm from 21st Divisional Inexperienced Brigade. Sections attained OISEMENT Station and were conveyed hence by Pontoon wagons.	
"	20		No 3 Section instructor in Musketry and Rifle Firing on Range 9.0 - 11.30 am. Instruction in Lewis Gun to No 3 Section Team. Company bathed in Stream (LIGER RIVER) and washed Clothes.	
"	21		Company paraded 9.0 am and after inspection, ordered to Stand by in case of a move. Company paraded 3.0 pm. and marched to SORENG on la BRESLE River and billeted. Epidemic of Pyrexia (unknown origin) or Influenza in the Company - Some 15 Cases. An Orderly despatched to 63 Ambulance for Quinine.	

WAR DIARY
or
INTELLIGENCE SUMMARY.

Army Form C. 2118.

Place	Date	Hour	Summary of Events and Information	Remarks and references to Appendices
LORENG	JUNE 22		Company marched at 11.0 am to BETHENCOURT or L'YERES Rm. Arrived 1:30 p.m. and billeted. Sickness in Company on the increase. Sent for 63 Field Ambulance M.O. who came in the evening, taking away about 8 cases to Hospital.	
BETHEN-COURT	23		Company has mounted section parade 9.0 am. Exercised in section and arm drill. Box respirator drill. Section working together per section in Lewis Gun. Sickness still on increase. 9/4 men off after 11.0 am.	
"	24		Company has mounted section parade 9.0 am. Exercised in section arm drill. Box respirators and Physical drill, firing on Short Range. Lewis gun training discontinued owing to sickness in the Company. Commenced isolation of cases of sickness by use of a detached barn. Separate cook parade.	

Army Form C. 2118.

WAR DIARY
or
INTELLIGENCE SUMMARY.
(Erase heading not required.)

Place	Date	Hour	Summary of Events and Information	Remarks and references to Appendices
STEPHEN-COURT	JUNE 25		Company less Mounted Section paraded 9.0 a.m. No.1 Section working on new Bath House at VILLY LE BAS and locating position of Gas Shot-mark at J GUERVILLE and waterpoint at SEPT MEULES. Remainder Lectures instruction in Section and Arm Drill, Musketry including rifle practice on Short range. Games 2.30 to 4.30 p.m.	
			O.C. attending Company Conference under C.R.E. who laid down outline of weekly training programme. Two Officers and 20 men visited TREPORT during the day, going by motor lorry.	
"	26		Company less Mounted Section paraded 9.0 a.m. No.1 Section working on new Bath House at VILLY LE BAS. Located water point at SEPT MEULES and made preparations for Mooring Pump Engine. Remainder Lectures instruction in Section and Arm Drill, Musketry including rifle practice on Short range. Two Officers and 20 men visited Seaport at Le TREPORT during the day - Going by motor lorry.	
"	27			

WAR DIARY
INTELLIGENCE SUMMARY.
(Erase heading not required.)

Army Form C. 2118.

Place	Date	Hour	Summary of Events and Information	Remarks and references to Appendices
BETHEN- COURT	JUNE 27		Company less one Section and mounted parade 9.0 a.m. No.1 Section working on Bath House at VILLY LE BAS, with one Sapper at SEPT MEULES water point. Engine Pump in running order. Remaining Sections instructed in Section and Arm drill, Musketry including Rifle practice on short range. Two Officers and 20 men visited tea hut at le TREPORT during the day. Going by Motor Lorry.	
"	28		Inspection of Company billets 9.0 a.m. 9.15 a.m. Parade of Company less No.1 Section and Inspected. No.1 Section working on Bath House at VILLY LE BAS with one Sapper at SEPT MEULES water point. Remaining Sections instructed in Section and Arm drill, Musketry including Rifle practice on short range.	

Army Form C. 2118.

WAR DIARY
or
INTELLIGENCE SUMMARY.
(Erase heading not required.)

Place	Date	Hour	Summary of Events and Information	Remarks and references to Appendices
BETHEN-COURT	JUNE 99		Inspection of Company billets 9.0 a.m. 9.15 a.m. Parade of Company less No 1 Section and Dismounted. No 1 Section looking on Bath House at VILLY LE BAS with the Sappers at SEPT MEULES water point. Section and arm drill, musketry Remaining Sections instructed in Section and arm drill, musketry including Rifle practices on short range.	
"	30		Company Transport (less one G.S. limber) under Lieut CARNELLEY with 1st CLOUGH marched at 10.45 a.m. to join 62 Brigade Transport on march to OISEMENT. Arrived about 6.0 p.m. and billeted. Company, less Transport, remained BETHENCOURT	

James Trayn O.C.

WAR DIARY
or
INTELLIGENCE SUMMARY.
(Erase heading not required.)

Army Form C. 2118.

97 D Fld Co RE

Place	Date	Hour	Summary of Events and Information	Remarks and references to Appendices
BETHENCOURT	JULY 1		Company (less Transport) marched to GAMACHES - LONGROY Station LA BRESLE River. Arrived 7.45 a.m. and acted as loading party for 62nd Brigade Transport. Entrained troops M at 11.30 a.m. Entrained transport 6.30 p.m. and embused. Morage Transport marched to CANDAS. Arrived 11.30 p.m. and billeted. Morage Transport marched to BEAUQUESNE arrived 11.30 p.m. and billeted. Company Transport marched with bulk of 62nd Infantry Brigade Transport. Left OISEMENT 7.0 a.m., arrived BOURDON 1.30 p.m. & camped.	
BEAUQUESNE	2		Company (less Transport) paraded 2.0 p.m. for inspection. Company Transport marched with bulk of 62nd Infantry Brigade Transport. Left BOURDON 9.30 a.m. arrived HALLOY LES PERNOIS 2.0 p.m. and camped.	
"	3		Company Transport marched with bulk of 62nd Infantry Brigade Transport. Left HALLOY LES PERNOIS 3.0 a.m. arrived BEAUQUESNE 6.30 a.m. and rejoined Company. Box Respirator drill & section [illegible] from 9.30 a.m. to 10.0 p.m. Company standing by.	

Army Form C. 2118.

WAR DIARY
or
INTELLIGENCE SUMMARY.
(Erase heading not required.)

Instructions regarding War Diaries and Intelligence Summaries are contained in F. S. Regs., Part II. and the Staff Manual respectively. Title pages will be prepared in manuscript.

Place	Date	Hour	Summary of Events and Information	Remarks and references to Appendices
BEAURVESNE	JULY 4		Inspection of Billets 8.45 am. Section Instructed in Box Respirators, Lectures and Arm drill. Washed wagons after 11.0 am. Put into Tents to-day. 10th Field Company reinforcement 4 1 O.R. joined to-day from Base men of Co. who have many of them had slight injuries or suffering from PYREXIA of "Flu" Symptoms origin. Company put through gas chamber from 9.0 am. onwards. Games 2.30 to 4.0 pm.	
"	5			
"	6		Inspection of Billets 8.45 am. Company (less 3 Sections) paraded 9.0 am. and instructed from 9.30 to 1.0 pm in Section drill Musketry & Extended Order drill. Painting painting Steel Helmets and wagons pontoon Equipment etc.	
"	7		Company (less mounted section) attended Church parade during the morning. Three Officers and 2 Section Sergts attended demonstration at No. 7 RE Park ROSEL OF MOIR of "Pill Box" during the afternoon.	

WAR DIARY or INTELLIGENCE SUMMARY

Army Form C. 2118.

Place	Date	Hour	Summary of Events and Information	Remarks and references to Appendices
BEAUQUESNE	July 8		Inspection of Billets 8.45 a.m. Company (less mounted section) & No 2 & No 3rd Section paraded 9.0 a.m. No 3rd Section doing troop exercise. No 2 the Bn. 9.30 a.m. to 1.0 p.m. Lecture on arm drill, musketry. No 2 section working on Vaporator. Lecture & construction of Bath at RAINCHEVAL. 7.30 a.m. to 4.30 p.m. 2.30 to 4.0 p.m. Games	
"	9		Inspection of Billets 8.45 a.m. No 2 and No 3rd Section Company (less mounted section) paraded 9.0 a.m. No 1 Section Company (less mounted section) No 3rd section doing troop exercise. 9.30 a.m. to 1.0 p.m. No 1 section doing horse exercise. No 2 Section doing Bn. vehicles, Lecture on arm drill. No 2 Section working on Baths. RAINCHEVAL from 7.30 a.m. to 4.30 p.m. No 1, 3 & 4 sections bathed at BEAUQUESNE baths & Bn. & inoculated. Change of under clothing – shirts vest pants socks.	
"	10		Inspection of Billets 8.45 a.m. Company (less No 2 part No 4 and inoculated section) parade 9.0 a.m. No 2 part No 4 section bathed. No 2 section working on Bath at RAINCHEVAL. 7.30 a.m. to 4.30 a.m. Part No 4 section Corps Commander – situated look on MAGPIES NEST O.P. for Corps Commander – situated between LEALVILLERS and VARENNES. Remainder of Company including Transport inspected with 62nd Infantry	

Army Form C. 2118.

WAR DIARY
or
INTELLIGENCE SUMMARY.
(Erase heading not required.)

Place	Date	Hour	Summary of Events and Information	Remarks and references to Appendices
BEAUQUESNE	JULY 11		Inspection of Billets 8.45 a.m. Company paraded 9.15 a.m. Lectures N°. 1,3 & 4 Training. N°. 2 Section working on baths at RAINCHEVAL. Part N°. 4 Section working on Magpies Nest between LEALVILLERS and VARENNES. Bridging Equipment sent to N°. 7 R.E. Park ROSEL.	
"	12		Inspection of Billets 8.45 a.m. Company paraded 9.15 a.m. Section 1.30 p.m. Lectures N°. 1,3 & 4 Training. N°. 2 Section working on baths RAINCHEVAL, part N°. 4 Section working on Magpies Nest between LEALVILLERS and VARENNES. Lecture for Officers and NCOs during afternoon. Tactical Scheme	
"	13		Inspection of Billets 8.45 a.m. Company paraded 9.15 a.m. N°. 1, 3 & 4 Lectures Training. N°. 2 Section working on baths RAINCHEVAL.	
"	14		Inspection of Billets 8.45 a.m. Church parade service hours	
"	15		Inspection of Billets 8.45 a.m. Company paraded 9.15 a.m. N°. 1 & 3 Lectures Training. N°. 2 Section working on baths RAINCHEVAL. N°. 4 Section making Traverse at Horse Lines. Games during afternoon	

WAR DIARY
or
INTELLIGENCE SUMMARY.
(Erase heading not required.)

Army Form C. 2118.

Place	Date	Hour	Summary of Events and Information	Remarks and references to Appendices
BEAUQUESNE	JULY 16		Inspection of Billets 8.45 a.m. Company parade 9.15 a.m. No. 4 Section Training. No. 2 Section working on Paths. RAINCHEVAL. No. 1 & 3 Training making Traverse at Horse Lines. Tactical Scheme for Section making Traverse at Horse Lines. Officers & men during afternoon.	
"	17		Inspection of Billets 8.45 a.m. Company parade 9.15 a.m. No. 1 Section Training. No. 2 Section working on Paths. RAINCHEVAL. No. 3 & 4 Sections working on Traverse at Horse Lines. Games during afternoon.	
"	18		Inspection of Billets 8.45 a.m. Company parade 9.15 a.m. No. 3 Section Training. No. 2 Section working on Paths, RAINCHEVAL. No. 1 & 4 Sections working at Horse Lines. Sections making Traverse at Horse Lines.	
"	19		Company marched from BEAUQUESNE at 8.0 a.m. No. 1 Section going to ACHEUX. No. 2, 3 & 4 Sections to FORCEVILLE. Headquarters with mounted Section & Transport proceeded to CLAIRFAYE, arrived about 11.0 a.m.	

Army Form C. 2118.

WAR DIARY
or
INTELLIGENCE SUMMARY.
(Erase heading not required.)

Instructions regarding War Diaries and Intelligence Summaries are contained in F. S. Regs., Part II. and the Staff Manual respectively. Title pages will be prepared in manuscript.

Place	Date	Hour	Summary of Events and Information	Remarks and references to Appendices
CLAIRFAYE FARM	JULY 20		No. 1 Section working on BROWN LINE shelters No. 2, 3 Section making dugouts at FORCEVILLE. No. 4 Section working on M.G. Emplacement at P.24.b.2.4. west of ENGLEBELMER.	
"	21		No. 1 Section working on BROWN LINE. Building up and repairing parapets. No. 2 & 3 Section making Dugouts & Ammunition Recesses at FORCEVILLE. No. 4 Section working on M.G. Emplacement at P.24.b.2.4. west of ENGLEBELMER.	
"	22		No. 1 Section working on BROWN LINE as above. No. 2, 3 & 4 Sections working on M.G. Emplacements P.24.b.2.4; Q.25.a.5.6; Q19.B.9.5. Q.7.b.9.6; Q.7.b.5.6.	
"	23		No. 1 Section working on BROWN LINE as above and constructing SOLDER KILN at wood between ACHEUX and LOUVENCOURT O.6.a.2.3. No. 2, 3 & 4 Sections working on M.G. Emplacements as above. LIEUT G. V. SCOTT ordered to take on 2nd in Command.	

WAR DIARY
or
INTELLIGENCE SUMMARY.
(Erase heading not required.)

Army Form C. 2118.

Place	Date	Hour	Summary of Events and Information	Remarks and references to Appendices
CLAIRFAYE FARM.	JULY 24		No. 1 Section working in BROWN LINE and SOLDIER KILN Emplacement as above. No. 2, 3 & 4 Sections working on M.G. Emplacements as above. Company H.Q. closed at CLAIRFAYE at 3.0 p.m. and opened at FORCEVILLE at 4.0 p.m.	
FORCEVILLE				
FORCEVILLE	25		No. 1 Section marched to FORCEVILLE and joined No. 2, 3 & 4. Whole disposition at H.Q. Finished at 9.0 a.m. to BEAUSSART. Arrived 10.0 p.m. Mounted Section marched from CLAIRFAYE to Camp in Thinaval Section with transport marched via ACHEUX and LOUVENCOURT O.6.a.2.3. Work between ACHEUX and LOUVENCOURT O.6.a.2.3.	
BEAUSSART	26		No. 1 Section working in Advanced Forward Zone (BEAUMONT RESERVE and TITAN AVENUE) deepening trench, putting in firebays, preparing for trench mortar filling in HAZEL AVENUE & Remaining Sections working in Camp and preparing for taking on work to follow.	
"	27		No. 1 Section working in Advanced Forward Zone as above. " 2 " Tramway track around BEAUSSART and making trench gate. " 3 " mending dug Depot in BEAUMONT RESERVE near the BOWERY. " 4 " Constructing Motor Pill-Boxes in OCEAN LINE.	

WAR DIARY
or
INTELLIGENCE SUMMARY.

Army Form C. 2118.

Place	Date	Hour	Summary of Events and Information	Remarks and references to Appendices
BEAUSSART	JULY 28		No. 1 Section away to Reluf of Battalions in Forward Zone. " 2 " working on Trench Gabs, Notice Boards, Shelters, Dugouts and track control BEAUSSART. " 3 " Deep Dugout in BEAUMONT RESERVE and in R.F.A. dugout in BOWERY AVENUE. " 4 " Section on M.G.R. Pill Boxes in OCEAN LINE and strengthening MAILLY MAILLET MILL	
"	29		No. 1 Section working in Advanced Forward Zone, fixing Trench Gates, Gravens drainage &c. " 2 " Section working on Trench Gate, drainage of BEAUSSART SWITCH O.P. to 62 t Brigade Intelligence Officer. " 3 " Section working on Deep Dugouts as above. " 4 " TRENCHES as before drainage of OCEAN and BONNET which has become impassable.	

Army Form C. 2118.

WAR DIARY
or
INTELLIGENCE SUMMARY.
(Erase heading not required.)

Instructions regarding War Diaries and Intelligence Summaries are contained in F. S. Regs., Part II. and the Staff Manual respectively. Title pages will be prepared in manuscript.

Place	Date	Hour	Summary of Events and Information	Remarks and references to Appendices
BEAUSSART	JULY 30		No 1 Section working in Advanced Forward Zone as above.	
			2 " making Trench gates Shelter Dugouts in Camp OP. M62L	
			Brigade Intelligence Officer.	
			3 Section working on Dug Dugouts as above.	
			4 Section working on MTR Pill Attrs in OCEAN LINE and Shinglitump MAILLY MAILLET MILL.	
"	31		No 1 Section preparing for taking over M. G. Emplacements at ENGLEBELMER	
			2 " making (Measuring time) M. Circuit Motive Boards, Circuit	
			Seation and Shelter Dugouts in Camp	
			3 Section working on Dug Dugouts as above.	
			4 Section working on MTR Pill Attrs in OCEAN LINE and Shinglitump MAILLY MAILLET MILL.	

James Totten
Major RE
O.C. 97 Field Coy RE.

WAR DIARY or INTELLIGENCE SUMMARY

Army Form C. 2118.

97th Field Coy RE

Vol 36

Place	Date	Hour	Summary of Events and Information	Remarks
BEAUSSART	AUGUST 1		Nos 1 and 3 Sections commenced work on M.G. Emplacements A & B and C & D respectively in neighbourhood of ENGLEBELMER. No. 2 Section making Concrete Sections, Screens for Concrete work, O.P.'s for 62 Brigade Intelligence Officer and Stalk Dugouts in Camp. No. 4 Section in MOIR PILL Area in OCEAN LINE and SHEEPSKIN of MAILLY MAILLET MILL.	
BEAUSSART	2		Nos 1 and 3, 2 & 4 Sections working as above	
"	3		do.	
"	4		do.	
"	5		Company bathes — no work done	
"	6		Nos 1, 3 and 4 Sections working on M.G. Emplacement A,B, C & D in neighbourhood of ENGLEBELMER and MOIR PILL Area in OCEAN LINE and SHEEPSKIN MAILLY MAILLET MILL. No 2 Section making Stalk Dugouts in Camp, making Notice Board Sheepskin Dugout at 62 Brigade H.Q.	

WAR DIARY
INTELLIGENCE SUMMARY.
(Erase heading not required.)

Army Form C. 2118.

Place	Date	Hour	Summary of Events and Information	Remarks and references to Appendices
BEAUSSART	AUGUST 7		No 1 & 3 Sections working on M.G. Emplacements A B C & D in neighbourhood of ENGLEBELMER.	
"	8		No. 4 Section working on M.G. PILL BOXES in OCEAN LINE and Strongpoint MAILLY MAILLET MILL	
"	9		No. 2 Section working on Shelter Dugout in Camp, bending Reinforcement rods &c.	
"	10		do	
"	11		do	
"	12		No. 1 Section working on "A" Emplacement. No. 2 Section on "B" Emplacement; No. 3 Section on "C" Emplacement all in vicinity of ENGLEBELMER. No. 4 Section working on M.G. PILL BOXES in front of AUCHONVILLERS (Redoubt System)	
"	13		do	
"	14		do	
"	15		do	
"	16		Change of Clothing. Half Company bathe & receive	
"	17		do	

Army Form C. 2118.

WAR DIARY
or
INTELLIGENCE SUMMARY.
(Erase heading not required.)

Instructions regarding War Diaries and Intelligence Summaries are contained in F.S. Regs., Part II. and the Staff Manual respectively. Title pages will be prepared in manuscript.

Place	Date	Hour	Summary of Events and Information	Remarks and references to Appendices
BEAUSSART	JULY 15		No 1 Section working on "A" Emplacement, No 2 Section on "B" Emplacement, No 3 Section on "C" Emplacement, all in vicinity of ENGLEBELMER. No 4 Section working on M.G.R. Pill Boxes in front of AUCHONVILLERS and MAILLY MAILLET. No work during last night and no Infantry working parties.	
"	16		No work during yesterday — since 8 pm. No Infantry working as above.	
"	17		No. 1, 2, 3 & 4 Sections working as above. No Infantry working parties	
"	18		No. 1, 2, 3 & 4 Sections working as above. Shifts and late at 12 noon shift. No Infantry at 4 am. working as above	
"	19		No. 1, 2, 3 & 4 Sections working as above.	

Army Form C. 2118.

WAR DIARY
or
INTELLIGENCE SUMMARY.
(Erase heading not required.)

Place	Date	Hour	Summary of Events and Information	Remarks and references to Appendices
BEAUSSART	JULY 20		No. 1, 2, 3 & 4 Sections working on 4t 10 and 20 foot span bridges, pedal trestles, camouflets nets at VALLEY DUMP.	
"	21		Company paraded 9.0 am. and stood by standing by during the morning. No. 4 Section (pont) recruited MAILLY MAILLET cross roads flyly in the afternoon. 11 Corps. had commenced same. No. 2 & 3 Section under Lt CARNELLEY and 11th CLOUGH marched at 6.25 p.m. to work under Orders of 64 Infantry Brigade East of BEAUMONT HAMEL. No. 1 Section in Camp.	
"	22		No. 2 & 3 Sections put a footbridge across the ANCRE north of GRANDCOURT last night. No. 1 & 4 Sections standing by.	
"	23		No. 2 & 3 Sections working on footbridge across the Ancre S.W. of BEAUCOURT last night. No. 1 & 4 Sections standing by. Mounted Section moved from TEAPOT COPSE to inclosure between BEAUCOURT and BERTRANCOURT.	

Army Form C. 2118.

WAR DIARY
or
INTELLIGENCE SUMMARY.
(Erase heading not required.)

Instructions regarding War Diaries and Intelligence Summaries are contained in F. S. Regs., Part II. and the Staff Manual respectively. Title pages will be prepared in manuscript.

Place	Date	Hour	Summary of Events and Information	Remarks and references to Appendices
BEAUSSART	Aug 24		Company started work on Three Pack animal passages and the RIVER ANCRE west of GRANDCOURT. Two bridges over streams completed. No work began on crossing of marshes.	
AUCHONVILLERS	25		Work was completed on the three bridges and commenced on the causeways. The Company and the transport moved from causeways between BEAUSSART and BERTRANCOURT to AUCHONVILLERS	
BATTERY VALLEY near GRANDCOURT	26		Work was continued on 3 causeways over ANCRE which were made passable for Pack transport. Company & transport moved from AUCHONVILLERS to BATTERY VALLEY near GRANDCOURT and bivouaced. Reconnaisance party was arranged & twelve 1 officer & 6 OR examined & 1 German soldier.	
do	27		The work on the three causeways was continued and work was commenced on repairs to road from GRANDCOURT - THIEPVAL. A recce at LE SARS was reconnoitered. A further 10 OR were trained.	

D. D. & L., London, E.C.
(A10266) W+ W5300/P713 750,000 2/18 Sch. 88 Forms/C2118/16

Army Form C. 2118.

WAR DIARY
or
INTELLIGENCE SUMMARY.
(Erase heading not required.)

Instructions regarding War Diaries and Intelligence Summaries are contained in F. S. Regs., Part II. and the Staff Manual respectively. Title pages will be prepared in manuscript.

Place	Date	Hour	Summary of Events and Information	Remarks and references to Appendices
BATTERY VALLEY GRANDCOURT	Aug 28		Work was continued on GRANDCOURT – THIEPVAL road which was made passable for single horse transport. Light motor cars.	
do	Aug 29		2 Sections worked on improving GRANDCOURT – THIEPVAL road and made road passable for double Motor Transport. 1 Section worked on improving our RIVER ANCRE near GRANDCOURT. 1 Section worked on improving Pack Crossing over RIVER ANCRE west of GRANDCOURT.	
do	Aug 30		The Company worked on New bed of road at crossing over RIVER ANCRE near GRANDCOURT.	
do	Aug 31.		The Company worked on repairing MIRAUMONT – BEAUCOURT road making passable for Motor traffic both directions	

Army Form C. 2118.

97 "Field Coy R.E.

Vol 37

WAR DIARY
or
INTELLIGENCE SUMMARY.
(Erase heading not required.)

Place	Date	Hour	Summary of Events and Information	Remarks and references to Appendices
BATTERY VALLEY GRANDCOURT	Sep 1		Work was continued on the MIRAUMONT - BEAUCOURT ROAD also on the MIRAUMONT - COURCELETTE Road. The plant covering at MIRAUMONT BRIDGE was repaired	
do	Sep 2		do	
do	Sep 3		do	
do	Sep 4		The Company including Transport moved to LE SARS.	
LE SARS	Sep 5		Two sections moved to the 62nd Inf Bgde, attached for work. The Coy. HQ - two above two Sections and Transport - moved to MORVAL.	
MORVAL	Sep 6		Remaining two sections worked on Poulton Bridge over CANAL DU NORD	

Army Form C. 2118.

WAR DIARY
or
INTELLIGENCE SUMMARY.
(Erase heading not required.)

Instructions regarding War Diaries and Intelligence Summaries are contained in F. S. Regs., Part II. and the Staff Manual respectively. Title pages will be prepared in manuscript.

Place	Date	Hour	Summary of Events and Information	Remarks and references to Appendices
MORVAL	Sep 7.		Coy less 2 Sections moved to MANANCOURT. Transport moved from LE SARS to MANANCOURT. 6 O.R worked on bridge at SAULISEL. 2 Sections worked on crossings over CANAL DU NORD.	
MANANCOURT	Sep 8.		6 O.R completed worked on bridge at SAULISEL. Two Sections worked on near to MANANCOURT - ETRICOURT ROAD. Two pictures worked on repairs to MANANCOURT NURLU Road. 17 O.R worked on being into trough on NURLU - FINS ROAD	
do	Sep 9		4 O.R finished with tank & trough on NURLU - FINS ROAD. Two Sections worked on MANANCOURT - ETRICOURT - EQUANCOURT Rd & Two on MANANCOURT - NURLU - FINS ROAD.	
do	Sep 10.		The Coy worked on repairs to road, do on 9th, during the day, and on night of 10/11 worked at REVELON FARM making Strong Point.	

Army Form C. 2118.

WAR DIARY
or
INTELLIGENCE SUMMARY.
(Erase heading not required.)

Place	Date	Hour	Summary of Events and Information	Remarks and references to Appendices
	SEPTEMBER			
MANANCOURT	11		No 1 2 3 & 4 Sections worked night 10/11th on Strong point at REVELON FARM	
"	12		do	do 11/12th
"	13		do	do 12/13th
"	14		do	do 13/14th
"	15		do	do 14/15th
"	16		Company resting	
"	17		Company resting. Staff that will demand and 7 O.R. returned Company Photographed by photographic Section. Erection of 6 half length type Signal Shelters for a Brigade H.Q. at W. 22. c. 2.5. (Map 57 c S.E.)	

Army Form C. 2118.

WAR DIARY
or
INTELLIGENCE SUMMARY.
(Erase heading not required.)

Place	Date	Hour	Summary of Events and Information	Remarks and references to Appendices
	SEPTEMBER			
MANANCOURT	18		Company resting during daytime.	
"	19		No. 1, 2, 3 & 4 Sections worked night of 18/19th on 5 Posts South-west of VILLERS GUISLAIN	
"	20		Company resting	
"	21		Sections 1 & 2 making accommodation for 62nd Infantry Brigade S.W. of LE MESNIL EN ARROUAISE. Sections 2 & 4 re-constructing Autreppes Chateau in EQUANCOURT as Hd. Qrs. for 33rd Division	
"	22		do. do.	
"	23		do. do.	
"	24		Sections 1, 2, 3 & 4 commenced erection of Nissen Hut Camp for 21st Division Hd. Qrs. north of EQUANCOURT (V.4.b.)	
HEUDICOURT	25		do. do. Mounted Section and Hd. Qrs. of Company moved to W.9.c.9.3 (N. of HEUDICOURT) taking over the Camp of 77 Field Coy. R.E. (17 Division)	

Army Form C. 2118.

WAR DIARY
or
INTELLIGENCE SUMMARY.
(Erase heading not required.)

Instructions regarding War Diaries and Intelligence Summaries are contained in F. S. Regs., Part II. and the Staff Manual respectively. Title pages will be prepared in manuscript.

Place	Date	Hour	Summary of Events and Information	Remarks and references to Appendices
HEUDICOURT	SEPTEMBER 26		Company finished work on Nissen Hut-Camp for 1st Cho 21st Deptr.	
"	27		Company resting	
"	28		do. Dismounted patron taken at EQUANCOURT Baths.	
"	29		Lt CRINELLEY attached to 62nd I Brigade for reconnaissance of bridge on l'ESCAUT Canal. No 2 Section under L.DEMAINE also attached to same brigade to preliminary work on enemy's mines of l'ESCAUT Canal. Remainder of Company resting	
	30		As above except that O/C Transport moved to O.P. H.Q. at W.Q.e.9.2 N. of HEUDICOURT close to which place main body of Transport is located up with Brigade Stores.	

C O N F I D E N T I A L.

WAR DIARY

OF

97th (Field) Company., Royal Engineers.

FROM Oct. 1st. TO Oct. 31st 1918.

Original.

Army Form C. 2118.

97 (Field) Co. RE

WAR DIARY
INTELLIGENCE SUMMARY

(Erase heading not required.)

Instructions regarding War Diaries and Intelligence Summaries are contained in F.S. Regs., Part II. and the Staff Manual respectively. Title pages will be prepared in manuscript.

Place	Date	Hour	Summary of Events and Information	Remarks and references to Appendices
	OCTOBER			
HEUDECOURT	1/2nd		No 2 & 4 Sections worked at night S.17 BANTEUX. Infantry bridges across L'ESCAUT CANAL. Both sections had to stand much sniping from opposite bank of Canal. One cork float bridge was got across & a small patrol crossed & returned. Enemy seemed but both machine guns & work was stopped. Lt. H. CHARNLEY smartly wounded and one Sapper-both by rifle fire.	
"	2/3rd		Approaches to Canal reconnoitred at night and some work was done on these by No 3 Section.	
"	3/4th		Pontoon bridging equipment dumped during the night at BANTEUX. No 4 Section worked at 62nd I.B. Headquarters. No 2 Post Cart was worked on a Cemmo Canoe. No 3 Section made a 30-feet Span Foot-bridge at Camp & other work. To support footbridge handed over to 98 Fd. Co. RE.	
"	5		Two heavy pontoon bridges for Infantry in file and two cork float bridges placed across the L'ESCAUT Canal S. of BANTEUX during the afternoon.	
GONNELIEU	6		Company march from HEUDECOURT to R27.a.5.8. EAST of GONNELIEU. the NCO & 10 men worked on VILLERS GUISLAIN - BANTEUX Road opposite TURNER QUARRY. Remainder of Company billeted in Mill Cellar in Ruins in BANTEUX	

(A10260) Wt. W5300/P713 750,000 2/16 Sch. 32 Forms/C2118/10 D. E. & L. London, E.C.

Army Form C. 2118.

WAR DIARY
or
INTELLIGENCE SUMMARY.

(Erase heading not required.)

Place	Date	Hour	Summary of Events and Information	Remarks and references to Appendices
GONNELIEU	OCTOBER 7		Company Leggins two 20 men worked on BANTEUX Road and a division at Crater opposite TURNER QUARRY. Twenty men worked in Camp.	
"	8		Two Sections worked on Bridge near looks at BANTEUX and a Bridge approaches. Also Laked a field gun. 1/2 Section attached to 126 Field C/RE to look on Divisional H.Qrs. to Section removed both tyre from West of EQUANCOURT. One Company of Pioneers attached to look on BANTEUX Road.	
"	9		Two Sections worked on Bridges as above. One Section on Roads and one Section on division of Roads. Also Two Platoons of Pioneers attached to them for look on Roads - all look at BANTEUX.	
"	10		Company moved from GONNELIEU to WALINCOURT N.23.k.3.7. During morning Officer Open two men JCW air months light broken bridge across L'ESCAUT Canal at BANTEUX.	

Army Form C. 2118.

WAR DIARY
or
INTELLIGENCE SUMMARY.
(Erase heading not required.)

Instructions regarding War Diaries and Intelligence Summaries are contained in F. S. Regs., Part II. and the Staff Manual respectively. Title pages will be prepared in manuscript.

Place	Date	Hour	Summary of Events and Information	Remarks and references to Appendices
WALINCOURT	OCTOBER 11		No 2 Section worked on Aerial SEUGNY. No 3 Section worked on Bath House in WALINCOURT. No 1 & 4 Section worked in Camp.	
"	12		No 2 Section worked on Aerial SEUGNY. No 3 Section worked on Bath House in WALINCOURT. 12 Sappers worked on Divisional Theatre. Remainder exercised in Drill and worked in Camp.	
"	13		No 3 Section worked on WALINCOURT Bath House. 12 Sappers worked on Divisional Theatre. Remainder of Company and 12 Sappers worked on Divisional Theatre. Remainder rested during morning. Attended Church Parade during morning - rested during remainder of day.	
"	14		No 2 Section worked on hutts in SELVIGNY. worked at Divisional Theatre. Remainder of Theatre. Remainder in Section & Arm Drill. Physical Training of Small Box respirator. One N.C.O & 6 Sappers instructed in Section James during the afternoon.	

WAR DIARY
or
INTELLIGENCE SUMMARY.

Army Form C. 2118.

Place	Date	Hour	Summary of Events and Information	Remarks and references to Appendices
	OCTOBER			
WALINCOURT	15		No. 2 Section worked on huts. Remainder of Sappers exercised in Section I Arm drill. Box respirator and Physical Training. Sappers rested during afternoon.	
"	16		No. 2 Section worked on huts. SELVIGNY during morning. Sappers worked on Divisional Theatre. Remainder of Sappers instructed in Section I Arm drill. Box respirator and Physical Training. Company rested during afternoon.	
"	17		No. 2 Section worked on huts. SELVIGNY during morning. Sappers instructed in Section arm drill. Map Reading and Remainder of Company. Football match during afternoon.	
"	18		No. 2 Section worked on huts. SELVIGNY during part of the morning. Remainder of Sappers instructed in Section I Arm Drill or Company. moved at 15.30 hrs to AUDENCOURT, arriving at 19.00 hrs.	
AUDENCOURT	19		Company under orders of CRE 17 Division to construct a 12 ton Foot bridge across SELLE RIVER. Sappers experimenting with crib piles during afternoon.	

Army Form C. 2118.

WAR DIARY
or
INTELLIGENCE SUMMARY.
(Erase heading not required.)

Instructions regarding War Diaries and Intelligence Summaries are contained in F.S. Regs. Part II. and the Staff Manual respectively. Title pages will be prepared in manuscript.

Place	Date	Hour	Summary of Events and Information	Remarks and references to Appendices
AUDENCOURT	OCTOBER 20		No. 2 & 4 Sections worked on Construction of two Span Bridge 12 ton Cl II load across the River SELLE at NEUVILLY (K.8.a.7.8.) No. 1 & 3 Sections continued above during night until 00.30 hours on 21st when enemy SOS signal went up on the Ridge, shortly to sieve into M.G. & Machine gun became r.c.	
"	21		All four Sections (working 2 Sections at a time) worked on above Bridge completing it for traffic at 18.45 hours. One O.R. killed and 2 O.R. slightly wounded.	
"	22		Company attempt to came upon under orders of CRE, 21 Divn and rested. 34th	
NEUVILLY	23		No.1 Section paraded under orders of G.O.C. 62nd Brigade. No.2 Section worked on Construction of First Transport Bridge at VENDEGIES [F.7.c.6.7]. Company moved to NEUVILLY. [K.8.b.4.7.]. One O.R. killed.	
"	24		No.1 Section under orders of G.O.C. 62nd Brigade. No. 2 & 4 Sections worked on First Line Transport Bridge in front of VENDEGIES CHATEAU [F.13.a.8.7.] No 3 Section in Camp loading material for Bridges. No. 1, 2 & 4 Sections moved to VENDEGIES.	

WAR DIARY
or
INTELLIGENCE SUMMARY

Army Form C. 2118.

Place	Date	Hour	Summary of Events and Information	Remarks and references to Appendices
NEUVILLY	OCTOBER 25		No. 1 Section under Adv. G.O.C. 62nd Brigade. No. 2nd Section diamantled First line transport Bridge at VENDEGIES [F.7.e.6.] and replaced it by a 12 ton Ark-ton Bridge. No. 3 Section in Camp training & taking instruction &c.	
"	26		No. 1 Section as above. No. 2 Section finished First line Bridge in front of VENDEGIES Chateau [F.13.a.8.] No. 3 Section worked on 9.20 D.W. H.Q. and Dig Master at Indilge Chateau & erected 9 horse troughs along HARPIES RIVER.	
"	27		No. 1 Section worked on Bath House PONT du NORD. No. 2 Section rested. No. 3 Section worked on 2nd Div. H.Q. and Div. Master. No. 4 Section erected Horse troughs along HARPIES RIVER.	

WAR DIARY
INTELLIGENCE SUMMARY
Army Form C. 2118.

Place	Date	Hour	Summary of Events and Information	Remarks and references to Appendices
NEUVILLY	OCTOBER 28		No.1 Section rested. No.2 Section instructs in section and two drill for Personnel. Physical training. No.3 Section worked at Div Theatre. Clones R.E. Stores etc. No.4 Section worked on horse troughs etc. HARPIES RIVER	
"	29		Company moved to POIX DU NORD with transport at VENDEGIES AU BOIS. Company Outpost 4 O.R. killed 7 O.R. wounded during the night. Gun Poix du Nord was heavily shelled.	
POIX DU NORD	30		No.1 Section attached 62nd Infantry Brigade. Night 30/31st - One Section worked on thirty cwt Bridge Sect of POIX DU NORD, One Section preparing digging & preparing bridge of Pincers west of PINCERS. Twenty Fascines for Pincers by PETIT GAY FARM.	
"	31		No.1 Section attached 62nd Infantry Brigade. One Section put in trestle bridge 12 ft cable tred bridge at VENDEGIES AU BOIS to take up to tanks. NIGHT 31 Oct/1 November. Two Section carryg Fish Plates & up to Cross. Night - bed of PETIT GAY FARM and placing them ready to give into Gun Emplacmt. Repaired M.G. Gun Emplacmt Kendo to other hide Gun Emplacmt as...	

Confidential

Original

War Diary
of
M (Ned) Cobb

Month — November 1918.

VOL XXXIX

WAR DIARY or INTELLIGENCE SUMMARY

Army Form C. 2118.

Place	Date	Hour	Summary of Events and Information	Remarks and references to Appendices
POIX DU NORD	NOVEMBER 1		One Section attached to 62nd Infantry Brigade. 12 Tin Well Bridge at VENDEGIES AU BOIS completes as a Bridge to take Tanks. NCW 1/2 Norwich. Informed one Company of Pioneers deployed Assembly Trenches on west side of Stream near PETIT GAY FARM. One Section improving Starp Poste East of POIX DU NORD.	
"	2		Section attached to 62nd Bde. Coy moved to Bivouacs west of DURES WOOD, VENDEGIES AU BOIS	
"	3		Coy rested	
"	4		Coy moved again to POIX DU NORD. One Section attached to 62nd Infantry Brigade. Two Companies of Pioneers and one Section each from 98 Field Coy RE and our Coy marched to FORET DE MORMAL truck on Roads. Only one Coy of Pioneers plus 20 to were required. Remainder returned to their Camp	

WAR DIARY or INTELLIGENCE SUMMARY

Army Form C. 2118.

Place	Date	Hour	Summary of Events and Information	Remarks and references to Appendices
	November			
PONT du NORD	5		Coy moved to LOCQUIGNOL. One section attached to 62nd Infantry Brigade. Three sections and one Coy Pioneers normally attached to 2nd Brigade worked on the Craters at LOCQUIGNOL and roads in that vicinity.	
LOCQUIGNOL	6		Section returned to Coy from 62nd Infantry Brigade and rested. Three sections and one Coy Pioneers worked on the Craters at LOCQUIGNOL and roads in that vicinity. Timber Causeway across Crater finished 00.30 hrs 7/11/18. One section attached to 77	
"	7		Coy moved to LA TÊTE NOIRE. Field Coy RE.	
LA TÊTE NOIRE	8		Coy moved to BERLAIMONT, and worked on Approaches to prepared Heavy Trestle bridge across the SAMBRE CANAL.	
BERLAIMONT	9		Coy worked on Approaches to prepared Heavy Trestle Bridge on SAMBRE & Approaches to prepared Heavy Trestle Bridge on SAMBRE Canal Pioneers assisting.	

Army Form C. 2118.

WAR DIARY
or
INTELLIGENCE SUMMARY.

(Erase heading not required.)

Place	Date	Hour	Summary of Events and Information	Remarks and references to Appendices
BERLAIMONT	10		Coy worked on Heavy Trestle Bridge on SAMBRE CANAL. Platoons assisting at the Approaches.	Two Platoons One Platoon/Pioneers assisting.
"	11		Do.	
"	12		Do.	
"	13		Do.	
"	14		Do.	
"	15		Do.	
"	16		Do.	
"	17		Coy worked on Heavy Trestle Bridge on SAMBRE CANAL (BERLAIMONT) Completing handrail & approaches. Bridge opened for Traffic at 10.00 hours. Coy rested remainder of day. Half Platoon Pioneers working on Approaches from 07.00 to 12.00 hours	

WAR DIARY
INTELLIGENCE SUMMARY.

Army Form C. 2118.

Place	Date	Hour	Summary of Events and Information	Remarks and references to Appendices
BERLAIMONT	18		No 1 Section working on Division Theatre & for 62nd L. Brigade. Remaining Sections renewing Pontoon bridge on Sambre River at BERLAIMONT. Strengthening Handrail & putting up screening material on Heavy Trestle bridge.	
"	19		No 1 Section worked on Divisional Theatre & for 62nd L. Brigade. Remaining Sections renewing Pontoon Bridge on Sambre River at BERLAIMONT. Strengthening Handrail & putting up screening material on Heavy Trestle bridge. Rested during afternoon.	
"	20		Got rested and rested.	
"	21		C.M. removed Trestle Pontoon Bridge on the SAMBRE CANAL & re-arranged R.E. material near Heavy Trestle bridge	
"	22		Do. do. No 1 Section made footbridge. Took place of Trestle bridge renewal No 2 Section. Ammunition etc. near LA GRANDE CARRIERE.	

WAR DIARY
or
INTELLIGENCE SUMMARY.
(Erase heading not required.)

Army Form C. 2118.

Place	Date	Hour	Summary of Events and Information	Remarks and references to Appendices
BERLAIMONT	NOVEMBER 23		No. 1, 3 & 4 Sections instructed in Section & Arm Drill Bombing Musketry and Physical Training. No. 2 Section doing Ammunition Fatigue during the afternoon.	
"	24		No. 1 & 2 Sections went for a Route March. No. 4 Section doing Ammunition and Jumping Battles from AYMERIES. No. 3 Section Salving Football Boots & dump the afternoon.	
"	25		No. 1 Section worked on a Footbridge on the Oye-pean Channel at BERLAIMONT LOCKS. No. 2 Section salving R.E. Material. No. 3 Section salved Ammunition at LA GRANDE CARRIERE. No. 4 Section worked in Camp.	
"	26		No. 1 Section worked on a footbridge over the Oye-pean Channel at BERLAIMONT LOCKS. No. 2 Section salved Ammunition at LA GRANDE CARRIERE. No. 3 Salvg R.E. material from men. No. 4 Section Bridge & Tpt Bridge. No. 4 Section Chased Equipment.	

Army Form C. 2118.

WAR DIARY
or
INTELLIGENCE SUMMARY.
(Erase heading not required.)

Place	Date	Hour	Summary of Events and Information	Remarks and references to Appendices
BERLAIMONT	NOVEMBER 27		No. 1 Section completed Anchorage on the tow-pass Channel of BERLAIMONT LOCKS (EAST OF CANAL). Remaining Sections instructed in Squad drill & Physical Training. Squad and afternoon.	
"	28		Company bathed. No. 1 Section worked on material for Rugby Goal posts for 62nd Brigade. Remainder rested.	
"	29		No. 1 Section erected Rugby Goal posts for 62nd Brigade. Remaining Sections instructed in Squad drill without Arms. Arm drill and Rests during afternoon. Lecture Physical Training	
"	30		Coy Transport moved off at 09.00 hours (with 98 and 128 Coys Transport) on trek stage of March to CAVILLON Area. Cyclists accompanied Transport. Near R.S. Dons a Command accompanied by 11 Lt R.S. CAHN. Remainder of Coy worked in Camp &c	

James Potter Major RE
O.C. M Fld Coy RE

CONFIDENTIAL   ORIGINAL

WAR DIARY

of

97 (Field) Coy R.E.

Month of December 1918

Army Form C. 2118.

WAR DIARY
or
INTELLIGENCE SUMMARY.
(Erase heading not required.)

Instructions regarding War Diaries and Intelligence Summaries are contained in F. S. Regs., Part II. and the Staff Manual respectively. Title pages will be prepared in manuscript.

Place	Date	Hour	Summary of Events and Information	Remarks and references to Appendices
	DECEMBER			
BERLAIMONT	1		Company (less Transport and Cyclists) marched to ENGLEFONTAINE and billets there. Transport and Cyclists having reached NEUVILLY and billets last night moved on to VILLERS OUTREAUX and billets.	
ENGLEFONTAINE	2		Company (less Transport & Cyclists) marched to SLIESCHES STATION and entrained for AMIENS. Transport & Cyclists moved from VILLERS OUTREAUX to Outskirts of BUIRE.	
AMIENS	3		Company (less Transport & Cyclists) detrained AMIENS STATION and marched to CAVILLON and billets. Transport & Cyclists moved from BUIRE to PROYART	
CAVILLON	4		Company (less Transport & Cyclists) in billets. Transport & Cyclists moved from PROYART to GLISY.	
"	5		Company (less Transport & Cyclists) instruction & drill &c. Early morning Transport & Cyclists marched from GLISY to CAVILLON.	

Army Form C. 2118.

WAR DIARY
or
INTELLIGENCE SUMMARY.
(Erase heading not required.)

Instructions regarding War Diaries and Intelligence Summaries are contained in F.S. Regs., Part II. and the Staff Manual respectively. Title pages will be prepared in manuscript.

Place	Date	Hour	Summary of Events and Information	Remarks and references to Appendices
	DECEMBER			
CAVILLON	6		No 1, 2 & 3 Sections making roads in billets. CAVILLON; No 4 Section making roads at SAISSEVAL.	
"	7		Do. Do.	
"	8		No 3 & 4 Sections making roads at SAISSEVAL; No 1 & 2 Sections starting to building material.	
"	9		No 3 & 4 Sections making roads at SAISSEVAL. No 2 Section repairing toilets at PICQUIGNY. as No 3 looked a CAVILLON roads.	
"	10		No 1 & 4 Sections making roads and worked on CAVILLON roads. No 1 Section worked Equipment. No 3 Section worked on billets PICQUIGNY; No 2 worked on billets PICQUIGNY; No 4 Section worked on roads FOURDRINOY.	
"	11		No 1, 3 & 4 Sections worked on section of huts SAISSEVAL; No 2 Section worked on repair & building of billets to PICQUIGNY, work on attachment.	

Army Form C. 2118.

WAR DIARY
or
INTELLIGENCE SUMMARY.
(Erase heading not required.)

Instructions regarding War Diaries and Intelligence Summaries are contained in F. S. Regs., Part II. and the Staff Manual respectively. Title pages will be prepared in manuscript.

Place	Date	Hour	Summary of Events and Information	Remarks and references to Appendices
CAVILLON	DECEMBER 12		N° 1, 3 & 4 Section worked on erection of Huts SOISSEVAL. N°. 2 Section worked on repair of Billets at PICQUIGNY.	
"	13		Do.	
"	14		Do. As N° 9 Section moved to PICQUIGNY with attached to Platoon of Pioneer Company noted.	
"	15		PICQUIGNY N°. 4 Section moved to SOISSEVAL with Half Platoon 14 N.F. (Pioneers) Mixed for Attachment. Two Sections & PICQUIGNY to work with N°. 2 Section.	
"	16		N° 1 Section worked before N° 2 Section worked on erecting of Huts, erection of Nissen huts, Hut repairs to Bath Hours. Worked on erecting of Billets FOURDRINOY. N°. 4 Section worked on Section of Huts at SOISSEVAL. Two Half platoons of N.F. (Pioneers) Assisted N°. 20th Section.	
	17		16th Transport undertaken by C.R.E. Work as on 16th. Not B.W.	

WAR DIARY
or
INTELLIGENCE SUMMARY.

Army Form C. 2118.

Place	Date	Hour	Summary of Events and Information	Remarks and references to Appendices
	18th		No 1 Section employed at H.Q. afterwards returning to PICQUIGNY to work at LA CHAUSSÉE. Baths at PICQUIGNY completed. No 3 section worked at CAVILLON. No 4 Section at SOISSEVAL on hutting.	
	19		Nos 1 & 2 Section worked at PICQUIGNY & LA CHAUSSÉE & No 3 at FOURDINOY & No 4 at FOURDINOY.	
	20		— to —	
	21		PARIS Conference No 01/35. & No 10 & 2 Resting. No 3 & 4 continued as above.	
	22		— to — huge petto formed to	
	23		No 1 Section started work at BREILLY & continued at PICQUIGNY. No 3 & 4 continued as above.	

Army Form C. 2118.

WAR DIARY
or
INTELLIGENCE SUMMARY.
(Erase heading not required.)

Instructions regarding War Diaries and Intelligence Summaries are contained in F. S. Regs., Part II. and the Staff Manual respectively. Title pages will be prepared in manuscript.

Place	Date	Hour	Summary of Events and Information	Remarks and references to Appendices
	24		Working as above.	
	25		Xmas day. No work	
	26		No Section at BREILLY LA CHAUSSEE.	
			No Section at PICQUIGNY. No 2 Section moved	
			from PICQUIGNY. No 3 Section at FOURDINOY. No 4	
			Section at SAISSEVAL. Formed No 2 Section	
	27		No 1, 3 & 4 worked as above. No 3 section	
			worked at DAISSY CHATEAU.	
	28		do — do —	
	29		do — do —	
	30		do — do —	
	31		do — do —	

CONFIDENTIAL.

WAR DIARY

OF

97th (Field) Company R.E.

FROM:- 1st January 1919.   TO:- 31st January 1919.

War Diary.

Summary of Events &c.

Place	Date	
OISSY	Jan 1st	No 1 Section worked at BREILLY, LA CHAUSSEE & PICQUIGNY
		No 2 " " " Oissy & assisted at FOURDRINOY
		No 3 " " " Oissy.
		No 4 " " " SAISSEVAL
"	2	Major Fettes rejoined company 9 men of No 2 Section attached No 3 shifted to PICQUIGNY for work at LA CHAUSSEE. Sections continued work as above.
"	3	Company working on hutting for 67th Infantry Brigade. No 1 Section at BREILLY PICQUIGNY & ST PIERRE-A-GOUY
		2 " } FOURDRINOY LA CHAUSSEE.
		3 " } and OISSY
		4 " SAISSEVAL
"	4	Do Do Do

War Diary.

Summary of Events &c.

Place	Date	
OISSY	1919 Jany 5.	Company working on hutting for 62nd Inf. Bde.
		No 1 Section at: BREILLY, PICQUIGNY & ST PIERRE à GOUY.
		2 " } " FOURDRINOY, LA CHAUSSEE and OISSY.
		3 " }
		4 " " SAISSEVAL.
	6	" Do
	7	" Do
	8	" Do
	9	" Do
	10	Company working on hutting &c for 62nd I.B.
		No 1 Section at: BREILLY and PICQUIGNY
		2 " " LA CHAUSSEE & ST PIERRE à GOUY.
		3 " " OISSY and CAVILLON.
		4 " " SAISSEVAL SAISSEMONT & FOURDRINOY

Copy.

War Diary.

Summary of Events &.

Place	Date		
OISSY	1919 Jany 11th	Major Fetter M.C. departed for demobilization	Capt. H. de L. PANET R.E.
		assumed command.	
		Work as on 10th inst	
	12	Rest Day.	
	13	Work as for 11th inst	
	14	" " 13th "	
	15	" " "	
	16	" " "	
	17	Coy worked on hutting Jobs 62nd & 12 Area.	
		Nos 1 & 2 Sections PICQUIGNY, La CHAUSSÉE, St PIERRE à GOUY,	
		BREILLY.	
		Nos 3 & 4 SAISSEVAL, SAISSEMONT, BURDRINOT, CAVILLON.	
	18	Hutting 1st 62nd & R.d. Area.	
	19	Rest Day	
	20	Hutting 1/2 62nd & 1/2 R.d. Area	
	21		

War Diary

Place	Date	Summary of Events &c.	
OISSY	22	Hutting &c.	62" Inf Bde Area
	23	Do	Do
	24	Do	Do
	25	Do	Do
	26	Rest Day	
	27	Hutting &c.	Do
	28	Do	Do
	29	Do	Do
	30	Do	Do
	31	Do	Do

(Sd.) H. de R. Pinch.
Capt. R.E.
O/C. 91 Fd Coy R.E.

CONFIDENTIAL.

WAR DIARY

OF

97th (Field) Company., R.E.

FROM:- 1st February 1919. TO:- 28th February, 1919.

Army Form C. 2118.

WAR DIARY
or
INTELLIGENCE SUMMARY.
(Erase heading not required.)

Instructions regarding War Diaries and Intelligence Summaries are contained in F. S. Regs., Part II. and the Staff Manual respectively. Title pages will be prepared in manuscript.

Place	Date	Hour	Summary of Events and Information	Remarks and references to Appendices
Millencourt	1		Work on hutting 62nd Inf Bde Area	
	2		Rest day	
	3		Work on hutting	
	4		" " "	
	5		All Available Sappers moved to DREUIL to work on huts under 98th Field Coy R.E.	
	6		Work on huts at DREUIL lez AMIENS.	
	7		" " " " "	
	8		" " " " "	
	9		Rest day	
	10		Work completed. Detachment returned to Hqrs. at OISSY	
	11		Work on Camp at OISSY	
	12		" " " " "	
	13		" " " " "	
	14		" " " " "	

Army Form C. 2118.

WAR DIARY
or
INTELLIGENCE SUMMARY.

(Erase heading not required.)

Instructions regarding War Diaries and Intelligence Summaries are contained in F. S. Regs., Part II. and the Staff Manual respectively. Title pages will be prepared in manuscript.

Place	Date	Hour	Summary of Events and Information	Remarks and references to Appendices
ISSY	July 15		Work in Camp. ISSY.	
"	16		Rest day.	
"	17		Work in Camp. ISSY	
"	18		Do	
"	19		Do	
"	20		Do	
"	21		Do	
	22		Route Marche to OR & LONGARÉ to meet Cadre Comp.	
	23		Rest day	
	24		} Work in Cadre Camp arrived in	
	25			
	26			
	27			
	28			

W Storey Lt
a/c. 9 F.Coy R.E.

Army Form C. 2118.

WAR DIARY
or
INTELLIGENCE SUMMARY.
(Erase heading not required.)

Instructions regarding War Diaries and Intelligence Summaries are contained in F.S. Regs., Part II. and the Staff Manual respectively. Title pages will be prepared in manuscript.

Place	Date	Hour	Summary of Events and Information	Remarks and references to Appendices
OISSY	1-3-19		Work at Cadre Park continued.	
	2-3-19		Rest Day	
	3-3-19 to 8-3-19		Work at Cadre Park continued	
	9-3-19		Rest Day.	
	10-3-19 to 15-3-19		Do Do Removal of transport to Cadre Camp & Cadre Longpré completed.	
	16-3-19		Rest Day	
	17-3-19 to 22-3-19		Work at Cadre Park Longpré continued	
	23-3-19		Rest Day	
	24-3-19 to 29-3-19		Work at Cadre Park Longpré continued	
	30-3-19		Rest Day	
	31-3-19		Work at Cadre Park Longpré continued	

JoePainn Major RE
OC 97 Fd Coy RE

Army Form C. 2118.

WAR DIARY
or
INTELLIGENCE SUMMARY.
(Erase heading not required.)

Instructions regarding War Diaries and Intelligence Summaries are contained in F. S. Regs., Part II. and the Staff Manual respectively. Title pages will be prepared in manuscript.

97 X Coy R E
9 W 44
Clare

Place	Date	Hour	Summary of Events and Information	Remarks and references to Appendices
DOU	1.4.19		Work at Cadre Camp LONGPRE continued.	Clare
	2-4.19		Cadre paraded by march route to LONG-LE-CATELET (Somme).	
Long Le Catelet	4.4.19		Work at Cadre Camp. LONG PRE continued.	
	5.6.7.19		"	
	13.4.19		R.Hugo 2nd Lt. PAVEY R.E. seconded to 179th Field Coy R.E. reported and on 11.1.19	
	14.4.19		A/Capt A.S.DOIG R.E. took over command of 97th Field Coy R.E.	
	"		Vehicles & equipment inspected & found by L.D.O.S.	
	14.4.19		Preparing vehicles & equipment for entrainment	
	15.4.19		Baths at LONG.	
	16.		"	
	17.4.19		Entrainment preparations continued	
	18.4.19		"	
	19.4.19		Marched to LONGPRE and entrained for HAVRE at 15-30 hours	
	20.4.19			
HAVRE	20.4.19		Arrived at Havre 0500 hours and marched to Rest Camp.	
	27.4.19		Baths & preparations for embarkation	
	28.4.19		Loading of Transports on S.S. "Joanna"	
	29.4.19		UK. on S/S "Clack" entrained crossed to UK. on S/S "Clack"	

W Doig Capt
O.C. 97 th Coy R E Cadre

97th (FIELD) COMPANY R.E.

RANK.	NAME.	JOINED UNIT.	REMARKS.
Capt.	B.S. PHILLPOTTS.	27.10.14.	Promoted Major 30.10.14. Mentioned in C-in-C's Despatch June 1916. Wounded slightly 11.7.16 - Remained at duty. Awarded D.S.O. 4.1.17. Transferred to 38th Div as C.R.E. 18.9.16.
2nd Lt.	A.C. SPARKS.	4.11.14.	Promoted Temp/Lt. 11.7.15. Promoted a/Capt 6.11.15. Awarded M.C. 27.1.16. Appointed Adjutant R.E.21.Div. 4.6.17.
2nd Lt.	V. LOWE.	28.11.14.	Promoted Temp/Lt. 11.7.15. Wounded shell shock 26.6.16. Rejoined company 3.7.16. Mentioned in C-in-C's Despatch 15.8.17. Promoted Captain 18.9.17. To 1st Pontoon Park 15.12.17.
2nd Lt.	W.W. MARSDEN.	11.12.14.	Promoted Temp/Lt 11.7.15. Wounded H.E. 26.6.16. Rejoined company 1.12.16. To 126th Coy as 2nd in command 14.1.17.
2nd Lt.	G.E. HOWORTH.	11.12.14.	Promoted Temp/Lt 11.7.15. Appointed Adjutant R.E.21.Div 18.12.16. Rejoined 97th Coy. 4.6.17. To 214 A.T. Coy 1.7.17.
2nd Lt.	ELLIS.		Did not embark with company.
Capt.	K.S. PYNE.	6.15.	Transferred to be Adjutant 3rd Div.R.E. 5.11.15.
2nd Lt.	W.A. MC DONALD ALLEN.		Did not embark with company.
Interpreter.	THEILE.	9.9.15.	Transferred to French Mission G.H.Q. 25.10.15.

Rank.	Name	Joined company.	Remarks.
2nd Lt.	R.H. COLLYNS.	2.16.	Wounded H.E. 26.6.16. Rejoined unit 2.7.16. Promoted Temp/Lt 15.5.17. Mentioned in C-in-C's Despatch 1.1.18. Promoted a/Capt 22.3.18. Wounded, remained at duty 23.3.18. Promoted a/Major 27.4.18. Wounded 29.5.18. Died of wounds 1.6.18. Awarded M.C. 28.6.18. Awarded Legion D'Honneur 22.11.18.
2nd Lt.	R.Le Nestor.	5 or 6.16.	Wounded H.E. 26.6.16.
2nd Lt.	J.W. CLARKE.	6.6.16.	Wounded H.E. 15.7.16.
2nd Lt.	G.G. MC LEAN.	28.6.16.	Promoted Temp/Lt 24.6.17. Wounded H.E 22.4.18.
2nd Lt.	R. MC DONALD.	28.6.16.	Transferred to 126th Coy 23.3.17.
2nd Lt.	J.H. HORNBY	28.6.16.	Wounded 1.7.16.
Capt.	J.T. FIS-HER.	22.9.16.	Promoted Major 21.12.16. Awarded D.S.O. 31.12.17. Wounded 27.4.18.
Lieut.	D.H. JOHNSTON.	13.2.17.	Transferred to 126th Coy 4.3.17.
2nd Lt.	R.C. TOTTENHAM.	17.1.17.	Promoted Temp/Lt 12.5.17. Awarded M.C. 23.10.17. Wounded 1.11.17. Remained at duty. P.O.W. 22.3.18.
2nd Lt.	P.P. PAGE.	2.3.17.	Sick 16.10.17.
2nd Lt.	H. CARNELLEY.	24.3.17.	Promoted Temp/Lt. 21.4.18. Promoted a/Capt 28.5.18. to 22.7.18. Wounded 1.10.18. Awarded M.C. 3.11.18.
2nd Lt.	G.C. ROWE.	10.8.17.	Wounded 6.10.17.
2nd Lt.	T.E. MORGAN.	9.17.	Wounded & P.O.W. 22.3.18.
Lt.	N.J.C. FARMER.	12.12.17.	Promoted a/Capt 12.12.17.
2nd Lt.	G. BOOTH.	17.4.18.	Wounded & P.O.W. 22.3.18. Wounded 23.4.18.
2nd Lt.	E. CLOUGH.	17.4.18.	Hospital 11.9.18.
2nd Lt.	G. BOOTES.	20.4.18.	Hospital 7.8.18.
Lieut	J.D. FETTES.	26.4.18.	Promoted a/Capt 27.4.18. Promoted a/Major 28.5.18. Awarded M.C. 18.10.18.

Rank.	Name.	Joined unit.	Remarks.
2nd Lt.	H.H.ALLEN.	17.4.18.	Wounded 28.5.18. Returned 18.6.18
2nd Lt.	H. DEMAINE.	18.6.18.	Awarded M.C. 18.11.18.
Lieut.	G.V.SCOTT.	23.7.18.	a/Capt. 23.7.18.
2nd Lt.	R.S.CAHN.	3.9.18.	
Lieut	D.R.LYNE.	13.11.18.	

Rank.	Name.	Joined unit.	Remarks.
2nd Lt.	H.H.ALLEN.	17.4.18.	Wounded 28.5.18. Returned 18.6.18
2nd Lt.	H. DEMAINE.	18.6.18.	Awarded M.C. 18.11.18.
Lieut.	G.V.SCOTT.	23.7.18.	a/Capt. 23.7.18.
2nd Lt.	R.S.CAHN.	3.9.18.	
Lieut	D.R.LYNE.	13.11.18.	

Rank.	Name.	Joined unit.	Remarks.
2nd Lt.	H.H.ALLEN.	17.4.18.	Wounded 28.5.18. Returned 18.6.18
2nd Lt.	H. DEMAINE.	18.6.18.	Awarded M.C. 18.11.18.
Lieut.	G.V.SCOTT.	23.7.18.	a/Capt. 23.7.18.
2nd Lt.	R.S.CAHN.	3.9.18.	
Lieut	D.R.LYNE.	13.11.18.	

97th (FIELD) COMPANY R.E.

RANK	NAME	JOINED UNIT	REMARKS
Capt.	B.S. PHILLPOTTS	27.10.14	Promoted Major 30.10.14. Mentioned in C-in-C's Despatch June 1916. Wounded slightly 11.7.16 - Remained at duty. Awarded D.S.O. 4.1.17. Transferred to 38th Div as C.R.E. 18.9.16.
2nd Lt.	A.C. SPARKS	4.11.14	Promoted Temp/Lt. 11.7.15. Promoted a/Capt 6.11.15. Awarded M.C. 27.1.16. Appointed Adjutant R.E.21.Div. 4.6.17.
2nd Lt.	V. LOWE	28.11.14	Promoted Temp/Lt. 11.7.15. Wounded shell shock 26.6.16. Rejoined company 3.7.16. Mentioned in C-in-C's Despatch 15.8.17. Promoted Captain 18.9.17. To 1st Pontoon Park 15.12.17.
2nd Lt.	W.W. MARSDEN	11.12.14	Promoted Temp/Lt 11.7.15. Wounded H.E. 26.6.16. Rejoined company 1.12.16. To 126th Coy as 2nd in command 14.1.17.
2nd Lt.	G.E. HOWORTH	11.12.14	Promoted Temp/Lt 11.7.15. Appointed Adjutant R.E.21.Div 18.12.16. Rejoined 97th Coy. 4.6.17. To 214 A.T. Coy 1.7.17.
2nd Lt.	ELLIS		Did not embark with company.
Capt.	H.S. PYNE	6.15	Transferred to be Adjutant 3rd Div.R.E. 5.11.15.
2nd Lt.	W.A. MC DONALD ALLEN		Did not embark with company.
Interpreter	THELENE	9.9.15	Transferred to French Mission G.H.Q. 25.10.15.

Rank.	Name	Joined company.	Remarks.
2nd Lt.	R.H. COLLYNS.	2. 16.	Wounded H.E. 26.6.16. Rejoined unit 2.7.16. Promoted Temp/Lt 15.5.17. Mentioned in C-in-C's Despatch 1.1.18. Promoted a/Capt 22.3.18. Wounded, remained at duty 23.3.18. Promoted a/Major 27.4.18. Wounded 29.5.18. Died of wounds 1.6.18. Awarded M.C. 28.6.18. Awarded Legion D'Honneur 22.12.18.
2nd Lt.	R. Le Nestor.	5 or 6.16.	Wounded H.E.26.6.16.
2nd Lt.	J.W. CLARKE.	6.6.16.	Wounded H.E.15.7.16.
2nd Lt.	G.G. MC LEAN.	28.6.16.	Promoted Temp/Lt 24.6.17. Wounded H.E 22.4.18.
2nd Lt.	R. MC DONALD.	28.6.16.	Transferred to 126th Coy 23.3.17.
2nd Lt.	J.H. HORNBY	28.6.16.	Wounded 1.7.16.
Capt.	J.T. FIS-HER.	22.9.16.	Promoted Major 21.12.16. Awarded D.S.O. 31.12.17. Wounded 27.4.18.
Lieut.	D.H. JOHNSTON.	13.2.17.	Transferred to 126th Coy 4.3.17.
2nd Lt.	R.C. TOTTENHAM.	17.1.17.	Promoted Temp/Lt 12.5.17. Awarded M.C.23.10.17. Wounded 1.11.17. Remained at duty. P.O.W. 22.3.18.
2nd Lt.	P.P. PAGE.	2.3.17.	Sick 16.10.17.
2nd Lt.	H. CARNELLEY.	24.3.17.	Promoted Temp/Lt.21.4.18. Promoted a/Capt 28.5.18. to 22.7.18. Wounded 1.10.18. Awarded M.C. 3.11.18.
2nd Lt.	G.C. ROWE.	10.8.17.	Wounded 6.10.17.
2nd Lt.	T.E. MORGAN.	9.17.	Wounded & P.O.W.22.3.18.
Lt.	N.J.C. FARMER.	12.12.17.	Promoted a/Capt 12.12.17.
2nd Lt.	G. BOOTH.	17.4.18.	Wounded & P.O.W.22.3.18. Wounded 23.4.18.
2nd Lt.	E. CLOUGH.	17.4.18.	Hospital 11.9.18.
2nd Lt.	G. BOOTES.	20.4.18.	Hospital 7.8.18.
Lieut	J.D. FETTES.	26.4.18.	Promoted a/Capt 27.4.18. Promoted a/Major 28.5.18. Awarded M.C. 18.10.18.

Rank.	Name.	Joined unit.	Remarks.
2nd Lt.	H.H.ALLEN.	17.4.18.	Wounded 28.5.18. Returned 18.6.18
2nd Lt.	H. DEMAINE.	18.6.18.	Awarded M.C. 18.11.18.
Lieut.	G.V.SCOTT.	23.7.18.	a/Capt. 23.7.18.
2nd Lt.	R.S.CAHN.	3.9.18.	
Lieut	D.R.LYNE.	13.11.18.	

97th (FIELD) COMPANY R.E.

RANK.	NAME.	JOINED UNIT.	REMARKS.
Capt.	B.S. PHILLPOTTS.	27.10.14.	Promoted Major 30.10.14. Mentioned in C-in-C's Despatch June 1916. Wounded slightly 11.7.16 - Remained at duty. Awarded D.S.O. 4.1.17. Transferred to 38th Div as C.R.E 18.9.16.
2nd Lt.	A.C. SPARKS.	4.11.14.	Promoted Temp/Lt. 11.7.15. Promoted a/Capt 6.11.15. Awarded M.C. 27.1.16. Appointed Adjutant R.E.21.Div. 4.6.17.
2nd Lt.	V. LOWE.	28.11.14.	Promoted Temp/Lt. 11.7.15. Wounded shell shock 26.6.16. Rejoined company 3.7.16. Mentioned in C-in-C's Despatch 15.8.17. Promoted Captain 18.9.17. To 1st Pontoon Park 15.12.17.
2nd Lt.	W.W. MARSDEN.	11.12.14.	Promoted Temp/Lt 11.7.15. Wounded H.E. 26.6.16. Rejoined company 1.12.16. To 126th Coy as 2nd in command 14.1.17.
2nd Lt.	G.E. HOWORTH.	11.12.14.	Promoted Temp/Lt 11.7.15. Appointed Adjutant R.E.21.Div 18.12.16. Rejoined 97th Coy. 4.6.17. To 214 A.T. Coy 1.7.17.
2nd Lt.	ELLIS.		Did not embark with company.
Capt.	H.S. PYNE.	6.15.	Transferred to be Adjutant 3rd Div.R.E. 5.11.15.
2nd Lt.	W.A. MC DONALD ALLEN.		Did not embark with company.
Interpreter.	THÉIÈNE.	9.9.15.	Transferred to French Mission G.H.Q. 25.10.15.

Rank.	Name	Joined company.	Remarks.
2nd Lt.	R.H. COLLYNS.	2. 16.	Wounded H.E. 26.6.16.
			Rejoined unit 2.7.16.
			Promoted Temp/Lt 15.5.17.
			Mentioned in C-in-C's Despatch 1.1.18.
			Promoted a/Capt 22.3.18.
			Wounded, remained at duty 23.3.18.
			Promoted a/Major 27.4.18.
			Wounded 29.5.18.
			Died of wounds 1.6.18.
			Awarded M.C. 28.6.18.
			Awarded Legion D'Honneur 22.11.18.
2nd Lt.	R. Le Nestor.		
2nd Lt.	J.W. CLARKE.	5 or 6.16.	Wounded H.E. 26.6.16.
2nd Lt.	G.G. MC LEAN.	6.6.16.	Wounded H.E. 25.7.16.
		23.6.16.	Promoted Temp/Lt 24.6.17.
2nd Lt.	R. MC DONALD.	28.6.16.	Wounded H.E 22.4.18.
2nd Lt.	J.H. HORNBY	28.6.16.	Transferred to 126th Coy 25.3.17.
Capt.	J.T. FISHER.	22.9.16.	Wounded 1.7.16.
			Promoted Major 21.12.16.
			Awarded D.S.O. 31.12.17.
Lieut.	D.H. JOHNSTON.		Wounded 27.4.18.
2nd Lt.	R.C. TOTTENHAM.	13.2.17.	Transferred to 126th Coy 4.3.17.
		17.1.17.	Promoted Temp/Lt 12.5.17.
			Awarded M.C. 23.10.17.
			Wounded 1.11.17. Remained at duty.
2nd Lt.	P.P. PAGE.	2.3.17.	P.O.W. 22.3.18.
2nd Lt.	H. CARNELLEY.	24.3.17.	Sick 16.10.17.
			Promoted Temp/Lt. 21.4.18.
			Promoted a/Capt 28.5.18. to 22.7.18.
			Wounded 1.10.18.
2nd Lt.	G.C. ROWE.	10.8.17.	Awarded M.C. 3.11.18.
2nd Lt.	T.E. MORGAN.	9.17.	Wounded 6.10.17.
Lt.	N.J.C. FARMER.	12.12.17.	Wounded & P.O.W. 22.3.18.
2nd Lt.	G. BOOTH.	17.4.18.	Promoted a/Capt 12.12.17.
			Wounded & P.O.W. 22.3.18.
2nd Lt.	E. CLOUGH.	17.4.18.	Wounded 23.4.18.
2nd Lt.	G. BOOTES.	20.4.18.	Hospital 11.9.18.
Lieut	J.D. FETTES.	26.4.18.	Hospital 7.8.18.
			Promoted a/Capt 27.4.18.
			Promoted a/Major 28.5.18.
			Awarded M.C. 18.10.18.

97th (FIELD) COMPANY R.E.

RANK.	NAME.	JOINED UNIT.	REMARKS.
Capt.	B.S. PHILLPOTTS.	27.10.14.	Promoted Major 30.10.14. Mentioned in C-in-C's Despatch June 1916. Wounded slightly 11.7.16 - Remained at duty. Awarded D.S.O. 4.1.17. Transferred to 38th Div as C.R.E 18.9.16.
2nd Lt.	A.C. SPARKS.	4.11.14.	Promoted Temp/Lt. 11.7.15. Promoted a/Capt 6.11.15. Awarded M.C. 27.1.16. Appointed Adjutant R.E.21.Div. 4.6.17.
2nd Lt.	V. LOWE.	28.11.14.	Promoted Temp/Lt. 11.7.15. Wounded shell shock 26.6.16. Rejoined company 3.7.16. Mentioned in C-in-C's Despatch 15.8.17. Promoted Captain 18.9.17. To 1st Pontoon Park 15.12.17.
2nd Lt.	W.W. MARSDEN.	11.12.14.	Promoted Temp/Lt 11.7.15. Wounded H.E. 26.6.16. Rejoined company 1.12.16. To 126th Coy as 2nd in command 14.1.17.
2nd Lt.	G.E. HOWORTH.	11.12.14.	Promoted Temp/Lt 11.7.15. Appointed Adjutant R.E.21.Div 18.12.16. Rejoined 97th Coy. 4.6.17. To 214 A.T. Coy 1.7.17.
2nd Lt.	ELLIS.		Did not embark with company.
Capt.	H.S. PYNE.	6.15.	Transferred to be Adjutant 3rd Div.R.E. 5.11.15.
2nd Lt.	W.A. MC DONALD ALLEN.		Did not embark with company.
Interpreter.	THEIENE.	9.9.15.	Transferred to French Mission G.H.Q. 25.10.15.

Rank.	Name	Joined company.	Remarks.
2nd Lt.	R.H. COLLYNS.	2.16.	Wounded H.E. 26.6.16.
			Rejoined unit 2.7.16.
			Promoted Temp/Lt 15.5.17.
			Mentioned in C-in-C's Despatch 1.1.18.
			Promoted a/Capt 22.3.18.
			Wounded, remained at duty 23.3.18.
			Promoted a/Major 27.4.18.
			Wounded 29.5.18.
			Died of wounds 1.6.18.
			Awarded M.C. 28.6.18.
			Awarded Legion D'Honneur 22.11.18.
2nd Lt.	R. Le Nestor.	5 or 6.16.	Wounded H.E. 26.6.16.
2nd Lt.	J.W. CLARKE.	6.6.16.	Wounded H.E. 15.7.16.
2nd Lt.	G.G. MC LEAN.	28.6.16.	Promoted Temp/Lt 24.6.17.
2nd Lt.	R. MC DONALD.	28.6.16.	Wounded H.E 22.4.18.
2nd Lt.	J.H. HORNBY	28.6.16.	Transferred to 126th Coy 23.3.17.
Capt.	J.T. FIS-HER.	22.9.16.	Wounded 1.7.16.
			Promoted Major 21.12.16.
			Awarded D.S.O. 31.12.17.
Lieut.	D.H. JOHNSTON.	13.2.17.	Wounded 27.4.18.
2nd Lt.	R.C. TOTTENHAM.	17.1.17.	Transferred to 126th Coy 4.3.17.
			Promoted Temp/Lt 12.5.17.
			Awarded M.C. 23.10.17.
			Wounded 1.11.17. Remained at duty.
			P.O.W. 22.3.18.
2nd Lt.	P.P. PAGE.	2.3.17.	Sick 16.10.17.
2nd Lt.	H. CARNELLEY.	24.3.17.	Promoted Temp/Lt. 21.4.18.
			Promoted a/Capt 28.5.18. to 22.7.18.
			Wounded 1.10.18.
			Awarded M.C. 3.11.18.
2nd Lt.	G.C. ROWE.	10.8.17.	Wounded 6.10.17.
2nd Lt.	T.E. MORGAN.	9.17.	Wounded & P.O.W. 22.3.18.
Lt.	N.J.C. FARMER.	12.12.17.	Promoted a/Capt 12.12.17.
2nd Lt.	G. BOOTH.	17.4.18.	Wounded & P.O.W. 22.3.18.
2nd Lt.	E. CLOUGH.	17.4.18.	Wounded 23.4.18.
2nd Lt.	G. BOOTES.	20.4.18.	Hospital 11.9.18.
Lieut	J.D. FETTES.	26.4.18.	Hospital 7.8.18.
			Promoted a/Capt 27.4.18.
			Promoted a/Major 28.5.18.
			Awarded M.C. 18.10.18.

97th (FIELD) COMPANY R.E.

RANK.	NAME.	JOINED UNIT.	REMARKS.
Capt.	B.S. PHILLPOTTS.	27.10.14.	Promoted Major 30.10.14. Mentioned in C-in-C's Despatch June 1916. Wounded slightly 11.7.16 - Remained at duty. Awarded D.S.O. 4.1.17. Transferred to 38th Div as C.R.E. 18.9.16.
2nd Lt.	A.C. SPARKS.	4.11.14.	Promoted Temp/Lt. 11.7.15. Promoted a/Capt 6.11.15. Awarded M.C. 27.1.16. Appointed Adjutant R.E.21.Div. 4.6.17.
2nd Lt.	V. LOWE.	28.11.14.	Promoted Temp/Lt. 11.7.15. Wounded shell shock 26.6.16. Rejoined company 3.7.16. Mentioned in C-in-C's Despatch 15.8.17. Promoted Captain 18.9.17. To 1st Pontoon Park 15.12.17.
2nd Lt.	W.W. MARSDEN.	11.12.14.	Promoted Temp/Lt. 11.7.15. Wounded H.E. 26.6.16. Rejoined company 1.12.16. To 126th Coy as 2nd in command 14.1.17.
2nd Lt.	G.E. HOWORTH.	11.12.14.	Promoted Temp/Lt 11.7.15. Appointed Adjutant R.E.21.Div 18.12.16. Rejoined 97th Coy. 4.6.17. To 214 A.T. Coy 1.7.17.
2nd Lt.	ELLIS.		Did not embark with company.
Capt.	H.S. PYNE.	6.15.	Transferred to be Adjutant 3rd Div.R.E. 5.11.15.
2nd Lt.	W.A. MC DONALD ALLEN.		Did not embark with company.
Interpreter.	THEILENE.	9.9.15.	Transferred to French Mission G.H.Q. 25.10.15.

Rank.	Name	Joined company.	Remarks.
2nd Lt.	R.H. COLLYNS.	2. 16.	Wounded H.E. 26.6.16. Rejoined unit 2.7.16. Promoted Temp/Lt 15.5.17. Mentioned in C-in-C's Despatch 1.1.18. Promoted a/Capt 22.3.18. Wounded, remained at duty 23.3.18. Promoted a/Major 27.4.18. Wounded 29.5.18. Died of wounds 1.6.18. Awarded M.C. 28.6.18. Awarded Legion D'Honneur 22.12.18.
2nd Lt.	R. Le Nestor.	5 or 6.16.	Wounded H.E. 26.6.16.
2nd Lt.	J.W. CLARKE.	6.6.16.	Wounded H.E. 15.7.16.
2nd Lt.	G.G. MC LEAN.	27.6.16.	Promoted Temp/Lt 24.6.17. Wounded H.E 22.4.18.
2nd Lt.	R. MC DONALD.	28.6.16.	Transferred to 126th Coy 23.3.17.
2nd Lt.	J.H. HORNBY	28.6.16.	Wounded 1.7.16.
Capt.	J.T. FISHER.	22.9.16.	Promoted Major 21.12.16. Awarded D.S.O. 31.12.17. Wounded 27.4.18.
Lieut.	D.H. JOHNSTON.	13.2.17.	Transferred to 126th Coy 4.3.17.
2nd Lt.	R.C. TOTTENHAM.	17.1.17.	Promoted Temp/Lt 12.5.17. Awarded M.C. 23.10.17. Wounded 1.11.17. Remained at duty. P.O.W. 22.3.18.
2nd Lt.	P.P. PAGE.	2.3.17.	Sick 16.10.17.
2nd Lt.	H. CARNELLEY.	24.3.17.	Promoted Temp/Lt 21.4.18. Promoted a/Capt 28.5.18. to 22.7.18. Wounded 1.10.18. Awarded M.C. 3.11.18.
2nd Lt.	G.G. ROWE.	10.8.17.	Wounded 6.10.17.
2nd Lt.	T.E. MORGAN.	9.17.	Wounded & P.O.W. 22.3.18.
Lt.	N.J.C. FARMER.	12.12.17.	Promoted a/Capt 12.12.17.
2nd Lt.	G. BOOTH.	17.4.18.	Wounded & P.O.W. 22.3.18. Wounded 23.4.18.
2nd Lt.	E. CLOUGH.	17.4.18.	Hospital 11.9.18.
2nd Lt.	G. BOOTES.	20.4.18.	Hospital 7.8.18.
Lieut	J.D. FETTES.	26.4.18.	Promoted a/Capt 27.4.18. Promoted a/Major 28.5.18. Awarded M.C. 18.10.18.